BENJAMIN BAKER

FOREWORD BY NEAL C. WILSON

CRUCIAL
MOMENTS

TWELVE DEFINING EVENTS IN
BLACK ADVENTIST HISTORY

REVIEW AND HERALD® PUBLISHING ASSOCIATION
HAGERSTOWN, MD 21740

The author assumes full responsibility for the accuracy of all facts and
quotations as cited in this book.

Author's Note: The author has constructed narrative for each of the
Crucial Moments chapters. These narratives are based on the context,
historical times, and available materials. Direct quotations will be
referenced with chapter endnotes. Quotations not referenced are part of
the constructed narrative.

This book was
Edited and copyedited by William Cleveland
Cover design by Leumas Design
Interior design by Candy Harvey
Cover photo by Getty Images/Russell Thurston, Mark Anderson
Electronic makeup by Shirley M. Bolivar
Typeset: 11.5/14 Bembo

PRINTED IN U.S.A.
09 08 07 06 05   5 4 3 2 1

R&H Cataloging Service
Baker, Benjamin Joseph, 1979-
     Crucial moments: twelve defining events in Black Adventist history.

     1. African Americans—Seventh-day Adventists—History.
2. Seventh-day Adventists—African-Americans—History.   3. Seventh-
day Adventists—History.   I. Title.

                         286.732

ISBN 0-8280-1882-0

DEDICATION

To my father,
who is, above all else, an example.

ACKNOWLEDGMENTS

Sufficient gratitude can never be tendered to those who put you in a vantage position to write freely and earnestly. So many individuals contribute to a book, both directly and indirectly: directly through assistance and availability, indirectly through lives that inspire and animate the mind.

I would like to thank my father, Delbert Baker, whose previous books were the genesis of this project and who offered sterling assistance along the way. Eternal gratitude to my mother, Susan Baker, who labored tirelessly with me, believing fiercely in her son. To my brothers, David and Jonathan, who were always there for me. Thank you, Bill Cleveland, for your deft editorial work. Sian, you are the most unselfish person I know. Minneola Dixon, Joyce Williams, Kaven Ible, Jeannie Watkins—your help was invaluable. To my editor, Jeannette Johnson, you are wonderful.

Appreciation to all those who contributed to the ever-growing body of Black Adventist literature: Charles Dudley, Ciro Sepulveda, Ronald Graybill, E. E. Cleveland, Mervyn Warren, Steven Norman, Calvin Rock, Charles Bradford, Emory Tolbert, and others.

Finally, resounding applause to all of the pioneers whose stories make up this book. Their example is everything. And to the God who does all things well.

CONTENTS

PREFACE

The history of Seventh-day Adventism is rich with colorful personalities, captivating adventures, and crucial moments that spellbind the audience. These stories increase faith, breed courage, and lend significance to our lives. Most important, they testify emphatically that this movement is God-ordained and has been called into existence to herald the coming Christ.

In particular, the history of African-American Seventh-day Adventists is insightful. Their story is that of a people enslaved for nearly 400 years: subjugated, degraded, and dehumanized, yet who emerged with determination. Their story includes strife, sacrifice, and a civil war that divided the strongest nation on earth. Their story is that of a caring heavenly Father, who interposed directly to free His subjected people. And it is the story of a denomination that at first reluctantly accepted the challenge to evangelize Black people, but that finally, under the efforts of a few Spirit-filled individuals, initiated an evangelistic thrust that rocked the globe.

This book highlights 12 crucial moments in the history of Black Adventism. Too provocative to not be told, these stories are rich with radical faith, vehement boldness, and amazing fervency. Read of people who followed God's Word, held His hand, and did the unthinkable. Meet individuals who brought Bible promises to life by grabbing hold of them in the midst of danger and crises. Thrill at the courage of souls who stared death in the face and defied it. Then be inspired by men and women who loved people—all people—too much to let them perish without hearing God's truth. In all this, experience the liberating peace of the gospel.

As you read, be encouraged and inspired. But don't stop there. Let the same Spirit electrify you to finish the work of God on the earth.

FOREWORD

Most reasonable, open-minded persons learn, grow, and profit from new perspectives and interpretations of major historical events—and even controversial issues.

This fascinating book, *Crucial Moments*, by Benjamin Baker, is illuminating and somewhat shocking, but also faith-confirming in God's timing and providence.

I long ago discovered, as you will in this significant volume, that we are all members of God's family. And in Christ, we are truly brothers and sisters.

—Neal C. Wilson
Former President
General Conference of Seventh-day Adventists

Crucial Moments is good reading—good for the mind and the spirit. Anyone and everyone interested in the highlights of African-American Seventh-day Adventist history will treasure this book.

—Calvin B. Rock
Former Vice President
General Conference of Seventh-day Adventists

CHAPTER 1

Dilemma

1842: BOSTON, MASSACHUSETTS

WILLIAM ELLIS FOY, A BLACK MAN, RECEIVES VISIONS FROM
GOD CONCERNING THE SECOND ADVENT AND FAITHFULLY
RELATES THEM UNTIL HIS DEATH.

~

*"Then I said, I will not make mention of him, nor speak
any more in his name. But his word was in mine heart as a
burning fire shut up in my bones" (Jer. 20:9).*

"I CAN'T DO IT! But I must! I must! But I am a
Colored man! How can I stand up and speak with authority
with White people in the audience? The visions are so controversial . . . I-I . . ."

It was a cold Sunday afternoon in 1842. William Foy, a
tall, light-skinned Black man, stood stooped over a sturdy
oak chair, wrestling with God in prayer. He had been at it for
hours. The small, sparsely furnished room was hot. A wood
fire smoldered in an old iron furnace. The conflict in his soul
caused unnoticed sweat to stream down his face, soaking
through his attire. His knees were painfully sore from hours
kneeling on the hard wooden floorboards.

Foy felt as though he was being torn in two. Half of him
wanted just to forget the past few weeks and just go back to

being plain old William Foy. The other half knew that the vivid visions that refused to fade from his mind were from God and must be shared. It seemed, whether he wished it or not, that his life was about to change drastically. He fell again to his knees.

Just then a tapping sound was heard at the front door. Then again, louder this time. "Who could that be?" Foy muttered to himself as he arose hesitantly to answer it. His stiff joints creaked and popped the whole way to the front door. Foy pulled the door open, and a burst of cold air whipped him in the face, reminding him that it was still wintertime in Boston.

VITAL STATISTICS

Born: *William Ellis Foy*
Birthplace: *Augusta, Maine*
Date: *1818*
Parents: *Joseph and Elizabeth Foy*
Married: *Ann Foy, circa 1836*
Children: *Amelia, circa 1837*
Died: *November 9, 1893*

Three White men stood in the doorway, each of them smiling cordially at Foy. They wore heavy overcoats and dark suits. It was the pastor and two elders from the Bromfield Street Second Methodist Episcopal Church, several blocks down the street.

"Greetings, Brother Foy; how are you today?" said Pastor J. B. Husted.

"Greetings, Elder Husted, Brother Brown, Brother Robbins. Good day to you all. Please come in and have a seat." Foy led the men to three chairs in his modest living room. "Let me take your coats."

"Thank you, Brother Foy," said Pastor Husted, the pastor of the church. The three men sat down and began rubbing their cold hands. "It's good to get out of the cold." The men exchanged pleasantries with Foy for a minute or two; then the mood shifted to the purpose of the visit.

Foy searched the men's faces. They seemed anticipatory and hopeful. "What can I do for you gentlemen?" Foy asked quietly, wondering what prompted the visit.

"Brother Foy," Pastor Husted began, "we have heard about your visions. People are talking about your experience and are impressed with your sermons. We are convinced you have an important message to share."

Word around the Boston community was that William Foy had been receiving visions from God about heaven, hell, and the judgment. Many people had been present when he was shown the visions, and they attested that his experiences appeared authentic. Foy had preached throughout the Black community, but he hadn't spoken about the visions yet to Whites.

DID YOU KNOW?

William Foy was contemporary with the following Adventist pioneers: Joseph Bates (1792-1872), Hiram Edson (1806-1882), James White (1821-1881), Ellen White (1827-1915), J. N. Andrews (1829-1883).

Foy's heart started to beat faster. He got that unmistakable feeling in his gut that meant only one thing—God was providing a venue for him to share his visions.

The pastor continued. "We know you to be a man of godliness and integrity, so we want to invite you to come and share with us your experience and the visions you have received."

"Yes, Brother Foy," chimed in one of the other men. "We all want to hear what God has revealed to you."

Foy's head spun. He felt nervous and frightened. *I had just been praying, placing my feelings about what I had seen in my visions. Now here are these men asking me to speak at their church. God surely must have sent them. How can I decline a direct invitation from His throne to share my experience?*

"Yes," Foy answered, "I will share what I have seen with your congregation. When do you want me to speak?" Immediately the peace of God flooded his soul like ocean waves lapping the sand. He felt the approval of the Lord warm his soul as the weight of the past couple of weeks lifted from him.

The three men smiled, then Pastor Husted said, "Wonderful, Brother Foy. How does tomorrow evening sound?"

Tomorrow evening! Foy almost doubled over as hesitancy and anxiety again flooded over him. *Remember, if this is God's will, all will be well,* Foy tried to reassure himself. Marshaling all of his willpower, Foy ignored those negative feelings and responded bravely, "That sounds fine, Elder Husted; thank you for your kind invitation."

Joyously the three men rose and pumped Foy's hand vigorously. Pastor Husted embraced Foy; then the four men prayed a brief prayer thanking God for His guidance and asking His blessing on the upcoming meeting. They then exited as quickly as they had come.

It is recorded that William Foy received four visions. The first vision dealt with the saints' reward in heaven and the fate of the wicked. The second vision portrayed the judgment scene. The third vision concerned God's providential guidance of His people. The fourth vision's content is unknown.

As Foy closed the door, it dawned on him that he had committed himself to speak to a predominately White congregation. *What was I thinking? This isn't the way things are done. I am a Colored man. In the South my brothers and sisters are still in bondage, enslaved. Even here in free Boston race matters. And I am going to tell a congregation of White folks that I have been given visions from God! I could be lynched, beaten—I have a family to think of.* Still, Foy had promised the men, and even beyond that, he had made a commitment to his Savior.

That night Foy tried to sleep, but he couldn't. He thought about how far God had led him. God had given him the ability to speak with power. He had gained a reputation as a preacher of righteousness, fearless and eager to preach God's truth. God had entrusted him with what had to be important information, vital information. And the requirement to share what he had seen. *And here I am wavering again.* Foy suddenly felt ashamed. He thought of the great men and women of the Bible and how they faced adversity to share God's Word. *How can I do less?*

Ann, his wife, was worried sick about him. But she realized there was nothing she could do. This was between her husband and his God, and she knew better than to interfere. She tried to comfort her husband, but it didn't seem to help much. She drifted off occasionally, only to be awakened by her husband's tossing and turning.

When William Foy finally did doze off, his sleep brought no rest. He dreamed that he was in front of a huge crowd of critical White faces. He attempted to relate the visions that God had given him, but nothing came out. He had forgotten his visions. He began to panic as he searched for something to say. Some people in the audience began to snicker; then the whole congregation joined in, guffawing loudly. He was the butt of the joke. He had never been more humiliated in his life.

The dream faded, but Foy's fears remained. Foy watched through his bedroom window as the majestic winter sun made its way to the center of the chilled morning sky. For a brief moment he forgot about his promise to the pastor. He forgot about his fears. He thought instead of God's mercies, how they are new every morning, and he was encouraged.

Things will turn out for the good, he told himself. He had an up-lifting devotion and session of prayer with his wife, then arose encouragingly refreshed to face the new day.

All during that long day Foy maintained his cheer. But by afternoon, shortly before the meeting was about to begin, those nagging feelings of fear and doubt returned. The temp-tation to refuse the speaking engagement pressed in on him. The same as yesterday, except 10 times worse. Foy wrestled with himself the way Jacob wrestled with the angel on that fateful night when he feared that his entire family

LAND OF THE FREE?

Boston, Massachusetts, the city in which William Foy lived, was the only major American city in the 1840s where every Black person was free.

would be slaughtered by Esau. Questions swirled in his mind demanding to be answered. *How will people receive me? Will I be persecuted and reviled? How will they react to my race? Will I remember the vision? Will they believe me?*

Then Foy again heard a tapping on his front door. He opened it and saw a sight he would never forget as long as he lived. A group of about 15 church members stood on his porch, huddled together, puffs of cold breath coming from their mouths. They had come to escort him to the church.

God had done it again! Foy imagined that he saw Jesus, as in Revelation 3:20, standing at the door and knocking. *How can I refuse to answer?* Foy thought.

"Brother Foy, good evening," the leader of the band began. "We have come to encourage you and to walk with you to the church."

The church members seemed to be cognizant of his dilemma and were sympathetic. They had been sent by God to strengthen him. Foy almost choked up with emotion right there on the spot.

"Thank you, thank you, brothers and sisters" Foy managed. "I'll be out in just a moment."

Foy bounded up the steps and told his wife and daughter he was going. He then kissed them goodbye and left. They would come to the church later. Grabbing his coat and hat, he walked confidently out of his house and into the miniature sea of believers. "We have been praying for you," some said. "We can't wait to hear about the visions the Lord has given you," said others. Foy nodded, happy to be flanked by the saints, buoyed by their support.

Although the Methodist Episcopal church was only a few blocks from Foy's house, the walk seemed like Christ's walk from the judgment hall to Calvary. And it wasn't because of the cold. Foy and his entourage passed the usual houses, shops, and churches, heard the familiar sounds of bustling city life, but he didn't notice any of it. His mind was on the meeting. As he neared Bromfield Street, he felt as though he was entering a labyrinth of dread.

Foy couldn't believe his eyes when the church came into view. People were streaming into the 1,000-seat auditorium! Well-dressed people—men, women, a few Blacks, mostly Whites—were pressing into the sanctuary, trying to get a good seat. It was 30 minutes before the program, and already the people were coming. Foy was at once encouraged (God had brought so many out to hear about his visions) and discouraged (what if he messed up and they rejected him?).

Inside the sanctuary, anticipation permeated the air. Some people whispered quietly; others sat and meditated. It seemed that everyone was eager to hear what Foy had to say. Excitement buzzed throughout the sanctuary. They knew of

Foy's religious experience, his dedication to God; but what of the visions he was said to have received?

William Foy was ushered to the pastor's study. There he prayed a prayer of desperation. "Father in heaven, You have placed me here. I am not equal to this great task. You must take control of me. May Your will be done. Amen." Prayer had always been a part of Foy's life, and tonight would be no different.

"Brother Foy, good to see you." Pastor Husted stepped into the small study of the church and placed his hand on Foy's shoulder.

"Elder Husted, good evening." Foy was happy to see a familiar face and fellow preacher.

"May God bless you as you share what He has revealed to you."

"Thank you, Elder Husted. Can you begin the meeting with prayer? I want God's Spirit to be present in the assembly," Foy said.

"Certainly," the pastor answered graciously.

In the back of his mind Foy hoped that the gathering would turn into a prayer meeting. That the pastor would open with prayer, and then another person would be moved to pray, then another, and another, until the allotted time for the service passed and Foy would be off the hook.

Pastor Husted prayed with Foy, and the platform participants stepped out of the office and onto the platform in view of the expectant congregation. It was like the days of Jesus: many people, all pressed into a small space to hear a word from the Lord. Solemnity marked the assembly.

The congregation was invited to kneel. A hushed sound echoed throughout the church—the sound of hundreds of people kneeling before God. Pastor Husted began: "Our heavenly Father, we come to Your throne of grace . . . ”

As he listened to the heartfelt prayer, Foy heard a voice—mysteriously, comfortingly—speaking to him: *"I am with thee, and I promised to be with thee."* Immediately Foy felt a heaven-sent feeling of freedom and boldness. With newfound confidence he cast off all his insecurities and fears. He felt empowered to do what he knew God had called him to do. He felt like a new man. His heart began to burn with the fire of God's Spirit. He was no longer afraid of what people would think or say. He was bursting to share what God had shown him.

PROPHETIC ACQUAINTANCE

Ellen White and her father heard William Foy speak several times in Beethoven Hall in Portland, Maine. Once she sat near Foy's wife. Ellen White later said: "It was remarkable testimonies that he [Foy] bore." ★

"Amen." The pastor arose, and the people slid back into their seats. He motioned for Foy to begin.

All fear gone, Foy stood up and began to speak. His words flowed like rushing water over a falls. Foy remembered every detail of his vision. He had such perfect clarity that he was able to describe his experiences in a poignant, lucid manner. He felt convicted that God meant for the people to hear a description of every scene that he had been shown, and the more he shared, the better he felt.

The audience sat spellbound. Not one person stirred the whole hour that Foy spoke. His race, social conditions, religious background—all faded before the powerful spiritual synergy in the message. With bated breath everyone listened as he related his vision of the judgment, the glories of heaven, and the wonderful person of his Friend, Jesus. He spoke with perfect freedom, his words thrilling the hearts of the hearers.

A sense of awe penetrated the audience as Foy spoke of the crystal sea, the thousands standing, waiting to praise the glorified Savior. Though Foy did not describe himself as such, many realized they were in the presence of a modern prophet of God.

When at the end of his message Foy made a call for everyone present to give their hearts to Jesus, there were tears of repentance. Many responded to the call. Lives were changed. From that day until his death in 1893, William Foy was faithful to God's call.

At the dawn of Adventism three individuals received visions from God—William Foy, Hazen Foss, and Ellen White. Hazen Foss refused to relate his visions, losing out, as he said, on his eternal reward. Ellen White became God's messenger to the Seventh-day Adventist Church. Though William Foy ministered to congregations outside the Adventist Church, he was faithful to the message he had been given, sharing his visions of heaven and judgment scores of times to thousands of people. Ellen White heard Foy repeating his visions, and wrote that he had a genuine experience and that his visions were remarkable.

EQUAL-OPPORTUNITY GOD

God chose a representative from three different groups in America to relay His prophetic message: Whites (Hazen Foss), Blacks (William Foy), and women (Ellen White).

In the later years of his life Foy ministered in the rural community of East Sullivan, Maine, where his grave is located. Local records refer to him, saying he was a powerful preacher who loved to talk about the coming of Christ. On the tombstone of William Foy (in Birch Tree Cemetery, Ellsworth, Maine), is this appropriate epitaph:

"I have fought a good fight,
I have finished my course,
I have kept the faith,
Henceforth there is laid up
For me a crown of righteousness."

William Foy was faithful in relating his visions in a time when Black people were ostracized, jailed, or even lynched for doing things less objectionable. Foy endured persecution, ridicule, and scorn, but he was steadfast in his mission. His ministry took place during a pivotal time in our church's history. By relating his visions and exhortations, he strengthened and encouraged believers in the Advent, many of whom likely made that second step to belief in the

William Foy grave site

remnant church. His influence on our church will be fully known only at the Second Coming.

The ministry of William Foy teaches us that God uses people of all colors, creeds, gender, and age mightily in His cause. God understands their fears, sympathizes with their infirmities, and is patient with their struggles. He says simply, "Be willing." If we are willing, He will be responsible for the success of the calling. Those whom He calls He enables to complete the work assigned to them, often against tremendous odds.

SUMMARY

- From 1818 to 1893 William Foy lives in the New England states (primarily Massachusetts and Maine).
- Foy receives genuine visions from God.

- He is commissioned by God to relate them.
- Foy is faithful to the call and shares his visions with believers all across New England.

LIFE LESSONS

- God wants to use all people, regardless of age, color, gender, or creed, to finish His work.
- God will help us to overcome fear, prejudice, persecution, and any other obstacle in order to proclaim His message.
- Only answering God's call will bring peace and happiness.

FURTHER READING

Baker, Delbert. *The Unknown Prophet.* Hagerstown, Md.: Review and Herald Pub. Assn., 1987.

Bennett, Lerone. *Before the Mayflower: A History of the Negro in America.* New York: Penguin Books, 1966.

Burner, David. *The American People.* St. James, N.Y.: Stoney Brook Press, 1980.

Franklin, John Hope. *From Slavery to Freedom.* New York: Alfred A. Knopf, Inc., 1980.

Horton, James. *Black Bostonians.* New York: Holmes and Meier, 1979.

Loughborough, John. *The Great Second Advent Movement.* Washington, D.C.: Review and Herald Pub. Assn., 1905.

★ Ellen G. White, *Manuscript Releases,* vol. 17, p. 96.

CHAPTER 2

Angel on the Battlefield
1861: ST. JOSEPH COUNTY, MICHIGAN

MRS. WHITE RECEIVES A SERIES OF VISIONS IN WHICH SHE
SEES THAT GOD IS PUNISHING THE NORTH AND SOUTH
FOR SLAVERY THROUGH THE WAR, AND THAT
HE WILL MAKE SURE THE SLAVES ARE FREED.

~

*"Surely the Lord God will do nothing, but he revealeth his
secret unto his servants the prophets" (Amos 3:7).*

FOR AMERICA IT SEEMED the worst of times. For
years the evil institution of slavery, and the right of Southern
states to continue the practice, threatened the very existence
of the United States. The North attempted to dictate to the
South conditions under which slavery could continue, but
the Southern states refused to let the North make any alter-
ation to their lifestyle and livelihood. Southerners, they said,
must be allowed to continue just as they always had, and the
North must stay out of their business.

When on November 6, 1860, at the height of the turmoil,
Abraham Lincoln was elected president on a platform oppos-
ing slavery, it seemed the country was destined to come apart.
One month later, legislations in state after state voted to secede
from the United States. On February 4, 1861, representatives

from Alabama, Florida, Georgia, Louisiana, Mississippi, South Carolina, and Texas met in Montgomery, Alabama, to announce the establishment of the Confederate States of America. On April 12, 1861, Fort Sumter was fired upon, and the Civil War had begun. The two sides felt so strongly about these great issues that they were willing to go to war.

On July 21, 1861, the first Battle of Bull Run occurred. It was the first real major conflict of the American Civil War. A Union army consisting of 30,000 men, commanded by General Irvin McDowell, fought 35,000 Confederates under General Pierre G. T. Beauregard. The Union army, under pressure to crush the rebellion in the South quickly, marched toward Richmond, Virginia, the capital of the Confederacy. They met the Confederate forces coming north from Manassas, Virginia, a Southern base. The battle, one of the most important in American history, took place in northern Virginia near a stream named Bull Run, about 30 miles from Washington, D.C.

The soldiers were mostly untrained, and the battle quickly turned chaotic. The sky filled with bullets and cannonballs, as men moved about the sparse hilly terrain, striving to kill one another. One could hear shouts from the living and cries from the injured and dying. Each side fought valiantly and bravely. It seemed that the conflict would go on forever. There appeared to be only one victor in this battle—the grave.

The tactics were complex and sometimes confusing as each side tried to outmaneuver and outwit the other. At one point the Northern army began to gain the ascendancy. The Southern army was losing troops fast and was low on ammunition. Hundreds of soldiers died in the conflagration, which lasted for more than five hours (by the end of the battle, casualties would amount to 2,900 killed, wounded, captured, or missing for McDowell's army and 2,000 for Beauregard's). It seemed that the contest was about to end in a Union victory.

What happened next has confused historians and scholars alike over the decades since. The battle suddenly turned, and with a burst of energy the South started to overpower the North. Those who witnessed the sudden reversal were at a loss to explain the phenomenon. According to one officer, "the whole field was a confused swarm of men, like bees, running away as fast as their legs could carry them, with all order and organization abandoned. In a moment the whole valley was filled with [retreating soldiers] as far as the eye could reach."

Some attributed the South's spark to General Thomas "Stonewall" Jackson, who showed up with 9,000 reinforcements; others to the South's courage and fortitude. However, Inspiration presents a whole different reason.

Later in 1861, in vision, Ellen White saw the Battle of Bull Run. She recorded in no uncertain terms what happened that day. She was unequivocal that the reason the tide of the battle turned that day was that God directly interposed.

She described what she saw—which was invisible to humans—take place. A mighty angel descended swiftly from heaven on a God-appointed assignment. The powerful being streaked through the stratosphere, traveling at lightning speed, and landed in the beleaguered valley, in the midst of the devastating carnage. The majestic angel waved a robust arm backward in a seismic swoop. Pandemonium and confusion ensued.

It appeared as if the Northern army were retreating, but they really weren't. The Southern soldiers attacked them viciously, sure of victory. In mere minutes hundreds of unidentified bodies lay scattered about the ruined landscape. The air was rank with the smell of death. The North began retreating, with the Confederate Army in hot pursuit. The battle was over. The South had won.

After this debacle both sides realized that this war was a serious matter; it would not be easy, and it would not end any time soon. Both sides realized that this would be a war to the finish—neither side would give up willingly.

Ellen White had three crucial Civil War visions in which God revealed many terrible things to her. First, she predicted that the United States would actually have a war. When she first related the vision, she said that the fatalities would be awful, and that some who were hearing her that day would lose sons in the war. She was shown in no uncertain terms that God was punishing the nation for allowing precious souls whom He created and for whom He died to be enslaved. Both sides were guilty: God was punishing the South for perpetrating slavery and the North for allowing it to continue for so long.

"SURELY THE LORD GOD WILL DO NOTHING . . ."

Ellen G. White actually predicted the Civil War and its bloodshed and atrocities. After coming out of her vision of 1861, she says: "There is not a person in this house who has even dreamed of the trouble that is coming upon the land. There will be a most terrible war." [1]

Ellen White stated that God allowed the conflict to continue for an extended period of time to let each side know of His displeasure. None would escape His judgment on slavery. America tried to pretend that the main issue of the war was not the chattel enslavement of a whole race. But Ellen White stated succinctly that God would not let the North obtain victory until they acknowledged that slavery "alone . . . lies at the foundation of the war." [2]

The North acted very piously in regard to the war. The

government made national appeals to fast and pray. They claimed that they were acting righteously in the matter and that God was on their side. But she said that these calls were "an insult to Jehovah. He accepts no such fasts."[3] Why? Because slavery was not made the primary issue of the war. Once Abraham Lincoln acknowledged that slavery was the issue, on January 1, 1863, Heaven began to facilitate the North's victory.

As she articulated in her description of Bull Run, Ellen White was clear on the importance of her visions. She spoke of the distinct judgment of God on the United States—both the North and the South. Slavery was a grievous sin in the eyes of

MYSTERIOUS WAYS

Ellen White was shown in vision that God actually prolonged the Civil War to punish each side for countenancing the cruel institution of slavery. Many times, humanly speaking, the war could have ended either way. But each time God interposed to prolong the conflict.

God. He was going to free His enslaved people, the oppressed Black race—those millions of souls dear to His heart. He was going to free the slaves in America as surely as He freed the Hebrews from Egyptian bondage while simultaneously meting judgment on the nation that countenanced the wicked institution. God forever let the world know how repugnant slavery and human bondage is.

Ellen White also highlighted another dimension. She expressly states that Satan was personally involved in the Battle of Bull Run and the entire Civil War. The stakes were high, and the issues were dear to his evil heart. The devil loved this war—all wars. Why? Because during military massacres he secures souls in his grip eternally.

Ellen White provided insights as to how Satan sent his demons to imitate dead generals and appear to the living ones. Demons would mimic the gestures and peculiar traits of revered military leaders. These spirits communicated with both Union and Confederate generals. The demons would give strategies and plans that would ensure great loss of life. Thus deceived, the living generals would follow the advice of the spirits, and whole squadrons would be obliterated to the devil's delight. She writes, "He loves to see the poor soldiers mowed down like grass."[4]

Corruption was exposed in her visions. President James Buchanan, who preceded Lincoln, had let the South steal weapons so that they would be better prepared when the conflict arose. Great Britain was seriously considering siding with the South because of the benefits that the alliance could bring them. Also, many Union generals were sympathetic to slavery and the cause of the South, and actually murdered their soldiers through subtle means.[5] Because of all this, Ellen White predicted that America would be humiliated.

The lesson of the Battle of Bull Run is clear. The issues of the great controversy between good and evil were clearly drawn in this strategic battle. The stage was set—the nation would learn the lesson that slavery, bondage, and oppression are unacceptable in the sight of a holy God. It may have seemed like just a battle, but from the divine perspective, the Battle of Bull Run was the arena where God began His deliverance of the oppressed. He could only stand to see His beloved people enslaved for so long. He personally intervened so that the chains were pulled off.

SUMMARY

- God gives Ellen White three visions concerning the Civil War. He tells His people:
  1. He is punishing the South for practicing slavery

and the North for allowing it.

2. He will not fight on the side of the North until they declare that slavery is the issue.

3. Despite the interference of evil angels, He will free the slaves.

LIFE LESSONS

• God is directly involved in the history of this world and often interposes to fulfill His will.

• God countenances oppression and injustice for only so long; then He metes out judgment.

• The history of peoples and nations is directed by God.

FURTHER READING

Coon, Roger. *The Great Visions of Ellen G. White*. Hagerstown, Md.: Review and Herald Pub. Assn., 1992.

Heidler, David, ed. *Encyclopedia of the American Civil War: A Political, Social, and Military History*. New York: W. W. Norton and Company, 2002.

Hummel, Jeffrey. *Emancipating Slaves, Enslaving Free Men: A History of the American Civil War*. New York: Open Court Publishing Company, 1996.

Leckie, Robert. *The Wars of America*. New York: HarperCollins Publishers, Inc., 1992.

White, Ellen G. *Testimonies for the Church*. Washington, D.C.: Review and Herald Pub Assn., vols. 1, 5, 1911.

---

[1] J. N. Loughborough, *The Rise and Progress of the Seventh-day Adventists,* p. 236; see also pp. 235-237.

[2] Ellen G. White, *Testimonies for the Church,* vol. 1, p. 254.

[3] *Ibid.,* p. 257.

[4] *Ibid.,* p. 366.

[5] *Ibid.,* pp. 253, 363, 364.

CM=2

CHAPTER 3

"Our Duty . . ."
1891: BATTLE CREEK, MICHIGAN

ELLEN WHITE HAD A BURDEN FOR THE BLACKS IN THE
SOUTH WHO KNEW NOTHING OF THE SEVENTH-DAY
ADVENTIST TRUTH, AND SHE VOCALIZED THAT BURDEN
TO THE DENOMINATION'S LEADERS.

~

*"Cry aloud, spare not, lift up thy voice like a trumpet,
and shew my people their transgression and the house
of Jacob their sins" (Isa. 58:1).*

THE LITTLE 63-YEAR-OLD woman sat in her
chair with the lapboard writing. Lines resulting from years of
consecrated toil marked her face. Her hair was pulled back
plainly in a braided knot that hung over the back of her neck.
It was all done neatly, and only tinges of gray in it hinted at
her age. Her jaw was set decisively, and her eyes showed in-
telligence, determination, and compassion all at once. She
wore a flowing black cotton dress that in its day was standard
for widows to wear. The collar of the dress was white, and a
heavy metallic watch hung near her waist.

It was late winter in Battle Creek, Michigan, and the chill
of the season was still evident. Ellen White arose early every
morning, sometimes at 4:00 and 5:00 to pray, study, and
write. This morning she hadn't really wanted to get out of

bed. The 1891 General Conference session was being held in Battle Creek, and the brethren had used her to the fullest extent, scheduling her to speak almost constantly. Dutifully, she had delivered address after address, speaking and exhorting tirelessly. Now, this morning, all the sleep that she had missed out on was catching up with her.

Yet as Ellen White arose from bed she knew this morning was different. God had a crucial message that He wanted her to deliver to the denomination's leaders. This morning she would write it out. Nothing would stop her from doing that. Pausing to pray, she asked for God's guidance, not only for the church and its leaders, but also for clarity as she wrote out the message God had given her.

E. G. White at her desk

Ellen White wrote slowly and deliberately, not pausing even for a short break. Her thoughts were lucid and succinct, penetrating and pointed. God had graciously answered her prayer, and she knew that she must get the force and urgency of this message across to the brethren: it was of the utmost importance.

Sometimes Ellen White would pause and contemplate the situation under which she was writing. She would weigh words and stop to think if there was a better way to write what she wanted to communicate. But on this occasion everything was as clear as the light proceeding from the throne of God—she knew exactly what God intended her to write. The words flowed out beautifully and simply.

Once she finished writing, Ellen White felt refreshed. She held the papers in her hands, her face breaking out into a beautiful smile. This was God's urgent message for the time. The top leaders in the church needed to hear it and act upon it.

~ ~ ~

Ellen White lived in perilous times when it came to race relations. She was born in a country that had one of the cruelest, most degrading systems ever known to humanity: chattel slavery. Although Ellen White was born far from it, in Gorham, Maine, she still felt the reverberations of the satanic institution.

In the late 1850s and early 1860s the situation reached a breaking point, and America did what today seems inconceivable: it turned on itself and declared civil war. As the war progressed, each side took a definite stand on slavery, and the battle waged in earnest over that issue.

WHAT MATTERS IN HEAVEN

"The color of the skin does not determine character in the heavenly courts."[1]

The North won, and slavery was abolished. But after slavery, what historians call "a new form of slavery" emerged. The recently freed Blacks were discriminated against, and clandestine groups and secret militias formed to intimidate and exterminate them. They weren't allowed to mingle with or attend any White social gathering or institution. If that wasn't enough, laws that kept Blacks subservient to Whites were enacted. Blacks were often lynched as law enforcement turned a blind eye. Or they were simply murdered, and nothing— neither investigation nor trial—was done to punish the perpetrators.

Whites who spoke out against these dire injustices were ostracized and often subjected to harm themselves. They were vilified in newspapers and magazines. On a more personal level, family members, friends, and associates turned their backs on them.

Sadly, much of Christendom reflected society's attitude toward Blacks. Very little effort was put forth to evangelize the freed Blacks, nor were many schools established to educate them. Much too often Christians provided erroneous biblical justification for the racist attitudes of Whites. Churches remained segregated, and Blacks were denied entrance when they were audacious enough to try to worship with their Caucasian brothers and sisters.

This was the world that Ellen White was born into. But she reflected none of the prevailing prejudice against Blacks. Instead, she used her influence and force of personality to right the injustice done to Blacks. Throughout her life she never ceased agitating the issue of equality, and she merits consideration as one of the great civil rights activists of her time. A few windows into her life support that assertion.

SAME GOD

"The God of the white man is the God of the black man, and the Lord declares that His love for the least of His children exceeds that of a mother for her beloved child."[2]

The Fugitive Slave Act of 1850 required "all good citizens" to return runaway slaves to their masters and report any suspicious Blacks who may have been slaves. Ellen White vehemently and vocally opposed this law, stating that the "law of our land requiring us to deliver a slave to his master, we are not to obey; and we must abide the consequences of violating this law."[3]

The statement reflected her attitude toward slavery: she hated it with every fiber of her being. She spoke against the insidious institution whenever she could. Some of her strongest statements concern the issue of slavery: "The whole system of slavery was originated by Satan, the tyrant over human beings whenever the opportunity offers for him to oppress. Whenever he can get the chance he ruins."[4] And concerning the abuse of the slaves, she wrote: "All is written, all, every injustice, every harm, every fraudulent action, every pang of anguish caused in physical suffering, is written in the books of heaven as done to Jesus Christ. . . . All who treat His property with cruelty are charged with doing it to Jesus Christ in the person of His heritage."[5]

Before the Civil War God gave Ellen White a vision concerning the impending battles. He showed her the carnage of souls that would occur. Then the Lord told her in no uncertain terms why this great war occurred. God was punishing the nation for the institution of slavery: the South for practicing it, and the North for countenancing it.

THE BOOK OF LIFE

"The ignorant and the wise, the rich and the poor, the heathen and the slave, white or black—Jesus paid the purchase money for their souls. If they believe on Him, His cleansing blood is applied to them. The black man's name is written in the book of life beside the white man's."[6]

After the slaves were freed, Ellen White urged the denomination to labor for the now-free Blacks. They were to risk their lives by going to the South and evangelizing. If they could not do that, they were to dedicate their means to the cause and help out in whatever way they could. Over the years Ellen White herself donated large sums of money to the cause in the South, even getting in debt to help uplift Black people.

Mrs. White freely mingled with all people. Her ministry was cosmopolitan, and she visited several countries. She was known to champion the cause of disadvantaged ethnic groups in those places also. Throughout her life she was Christ-centered (focused on Christ), not ethno-centered (focused on ethnic background). She was also known to sleep and eat and pray and fellowship and worship with Black people without a second thought.

Ellen White was more progressive in her thinking on race than many are even today. How was this so? How did she develop and maintain such enlightened views?

No doubt Ellen White's birthplace, Gorham, Maine, was a major influencing factor. Maine had always been primarily a free state. In particular, the state of Maine was renowned for its progressive and humanitarian views and was home to numerous reform movements and freethinkers.

Ellen White's parents also had a major influence on her thinking and development. Robert Harmon and Eunice Gould Harmon were both from the New England area and had grown up in an enlightened environment. More than that, Ellen's parents were people of spiritual conviction and principles. They were members of the Methodist Church and were later disfellowshipped because of their beliefs in the second advent of Christ, propounded by William Miller. They taught Ellen and her siblings to stand for truth and principle though the heavens fall.

An unfortunate incident occurred when Ellen was 9 years old. While walking from school one day, a young girl hurled a stone at Ellen and broke her nose. Young Ellen was unconscious for three weeks. The experience left her debilitated, ill, and disfigured. Because of this tragic event, Ellen was unable to finish her formal schooling. This event helped her to understand and relate to the disadvantaged.

Ellen White was, of course, a woman. She lived during times when women did not share equal rights with men. Women couldn't even vote. All her life she had to deal with the discrimination that came with being a woman, and this also helped her to empathize with the unduly persecuted.

Ellen White was converted to Jesus during her early teen years. Love for her Savior helped her to love and treat all people equally. Not only did she love Jesus, but she looked for His second coming. Because of this, she was termed a Millerite. Millerites were ostracized and suffered heavy persecution before, and especially after, the 1844 Disappointment. This was yet another link Ellen White shared with Black people.

SLAVES OF SIN

"Whatever may be your prejudices, your wonderful prudence, do not lose sight of this fact, that unless you put on Christ, and His Spirit dwells in you, you are slaves of sin and of Satan."[7]

Ellen White was naturally caring and compassionate. Her personality made her sympathetic to the downtrodden. In her life she consistently helped any whom she saw in need. Countless people told stories of how she helped them materially, monetarily, physically, and spiritually when they were in need. This attitude was extended toward all people.

Finally, the mission of the Seventh-day Adventist Church influenced the way Ellen White related to Blacks. She believed that Christ created all people, died for all people, and was coming back for whoever accepted Him as their personal Savior. She believed that this gospel was to be shared with everyone, according to the three angels' messages.

All of these factors combined to make Ellen White a key figure in the salvation of thousands of Blacks.

~ ~ ~

Ellen White made her way up to the pulpit on March 21, 1891, in the Dime Tabernacle in Battle Creek, Michigan. The church was historic, grand in its proportions, and replete with Seventh-day Adventist history. Thirty church leaders sat in the vast sanctuary, poised in their chairs, sensing the solemnity of the occasion and the weightiness of what was to be shared.

As Ellen White surveyed the leaders, the love of Christ was in her eyes. She never stopped praying that God would send His Spirit to impress every thought upon the hearers and move the church of God to action as never before.

Everyone's curiosity was piqued when Sister White abandoned her usual style of delivery. Normally she would exhort them without any notes, relying on her keen mind and the Holy Spirit. But today she clutched papers in her hand, and as she began she was looking down at the manuscript—not at them. Surely it must be important if she was going to read it word for word.

WHO'S TO BLAME?

"If the race is degraded, if they are repulsive in habits and manners, who made them so? Is there not much due to them from the white people? After so great a wrong has been done them, should not an earnest effort be made to lift them up?"[8]

And indeed, Ellen White did have something important to read that day. It was a message she had tried to communicate to church members, but to no avail. They simply would not pay attention. Or they would give mental assent, but not act on it. Writing it as a testimony was not enough—the written word must be transformed into the spoken word.

Ellen White began, and immediately after the first sentence tension filled the air.

"There has been much perplexity as to how our laborers in the South shall deal with the 'color line.'"[9]

From that sentence on came what is perhaps the most inspiring, passionate, and compelling address she ever gave. It is a masterpiece of the pure gospel of Jesus Christ applied to a group of people who were neglected and hated at the time. The message was Jesus Christ speaking directly to His church, very much akin to Matthew 5, where Christ shocked His hearers by breaking down the walls of tradition and cherished opinions. The 30 leaders sat stunned as Ellen White calmly read her manuscript.

This powerful appeal can be summarized in the following:

1. Our example of how to treat Colored people is found in the Bible in the example of Jesus. "The Lord Jesus came to our world to save men and women of all nationalities. He died just as much for the colored people as for the white race." [10]

2. Jesus' situation on earth was similar to the situation of the Colored people. "The Redeemer of the world was of humble parentage. . . . He chose a life of poverty and toil. . . . He passed by the wealthy and honored of the world. . . . He dwelt among the lowly of the earth." [11]

3. All of us are brothers, having the same Father. Nothing makes us different from each other. "The God of the white man is the God of the black man." [12]

4. All are one in Christ Jesus. "The ignorant and the wise, the rich and the poor, the heathen and the slave, white or black—Jesus paid the purchase money for their souls. If they believe on Him, His cleansing blood is applied to them. The black man's name is written in the book of life beside the white man's." [13]

5. Unless you put on Christ, you are a slave. "God makes no distinction between the North and the South. Whatever may be your prejudices, do not lose sight of this fact, that unless you put on Christ, and His Spirit dwells in you, you are slaves of sin and of Satan." [14]

6. God freed the Blacks from slavery just as He did the Hebrews. "God cares no less for the souls of the African race that might be won to serve Him than He cared for Israel."[15]

7. The church is guilty of not evangelizing Black people. "Sin rests upon us as a church because we have not made a greater effort for the salvation of souls among the colored people."[16]

8. The church should begin to earnestly work for the salvation of Colored people. "We should educate colored men to be missionaries among their own people. . . . White men and white women should be qualifying themselves to work among the colored people."[17]

9. More is expected from those who have been favored by God with blessings and privilege. "Those who have been favored with opportunities of education

James and Ellen White

and culture, who have had every advantage of religious influence, will be expected of God to possess pure and holy characters in accordance with the gifts bestowed. . . . Let the privileged ones make the most of their blessings, and realize that they are thus placed under greater obligation to labor for the good of others."[18]

10. The grace of God is needed more than education or machinery to do this work: we must be consecrated.

"There is altogether too much dependence on machinery, on mechanical working. Machinery is good in its place, but do not allow it to become too complicated. I tell you that in many cases it has retarded the work. . . . You must have the grace and love of God in order to succeed."[19]

Persons reading this document are compelled to admit that this is not only an inspiring call to missionary work but also one of the clearest presentations of the gospel. Yet very few present that day acted upon what they had just heard. Copies were furnished to key persons present, and it was even published in a 16-page leaflet, but no one did anything about it. No efforts were made for the Blacks in the South, except for a very few cursory attempts.

NO LICENSE

"You have no license from God to exclude the colored people from your places of worship. Treat them as Christ's property, which thay are, just as much as yourselves. They should hold membership in the church with the white brethren."[20]

Later that year Ellen White responded to an urgent call by the church to go to Australia. Yet even from Australia she did not set aside her burden. She wrote article after article in the *Review,* urging the church to action. She wrote personal letters to people of influence, trying to get them to share her vision. Very few responded.

But God's Word never returns to Him void. In 1893 Ellen White's son James Edson stumbled upon his mother's 1891 appeal to the General Conference leaders. He emerged as one who would go on to hazard his life for its Spirit-filled contents. He set out with his partner, Will Palmer, the two of them living out the message of Ellen White. They fearlessly risked their lives, giving all they had to preach the gospel to the Blacks in the South. God honored them for responding to His call, and their team eventually met with awesome success.

Eventually others picked up the torch. Whites and Blacks labored diligently in the South, considering every soul a precious candidate for salvation. God rewarded their efforts also. Now there are tens of thousands of Black Seventh-day Adventists when once there were none.

Ellen White's persistence powerfully illustrates several lessons. First, one person can make a difference. Ellen White never shrank back, thinking that she could not have an impact. Instead she pressed forward, knowing that with God she could do valiantly. Next, Ellen White never let the rejection of her message discourage her to a point where she stopped sharing it. She expressed disappointment, certainly, but she pressed on despite her feelings. Finally, the example of Ellen White teaches us of the results of sticking to God's message and proclaiming it faithfully. Thousands of Blacks and peoples of every nationality that the reverberating influence of Black people has touched owe their salvation to God and His working through a woman with the persistence and determination needed to change lives.

SUMMARY

- The slaves have been freed for decades, and nothing is being done for them in terms of evangelism.
- God places a heavy burden on Ellen White to wake the church up concerning this matter.
- In 1891 she addresses the General Conference leaders about it.
- Her message is ignored; later that year she is sent to Australia.

LIFE LESSONS

- One person can make a difference.
- Never let rejection or people's reaction discourage you from sharing what God tells you to share.
- Doing what God says always yields eternal results for the good.

FURTHER READING

Baker, Delbert. *Make Us One.* Boise, Idaho: Pacific Press Pub. Assn., 1995.

Graybill, Ron. *E. G. White and Church Race Relations.* Washington, D.C.: Review and Herald Pub. Assn., 1970.

Knight, George. *Walking With Ellen White.* Hagerstown, Md.: Review and Herald Pub. Assn., 1999.

Sepulveda, Ciro, ed. *Ellen White on the Color Line.* Huntsville, Al.: Biblos Press, 1997.

White, Arthur. *Ellen G. White: The Lonely Years,* Vol. 3. Hagerstown, Md.: Review and Herald Pub. Assn., 1984.

White, Ellen G. *The Southern Work.* Washington, D.C.: Review and Herald Pub. Assn., 1966.

———. *Testimonies for the Church,* vols. 1, 7, 9. Mountain View, Calif.: Pacific Press Pub. Assn., 1948.

---

[1] Ellen G. White, *The Southern Work,* p. 11.
[2] *Ibid.,* pp. 11, 12.
[3] E. G. White, *Testimonies,* vol. 1, p. 202.
[4] E. G. White, *Manuscript Releases,* vol. 4, p. 6.
[5] *Ibid.,* p. 7.
[6] White, *The Southern Work,* p. 12.
[7] *Ibid.,* p. 13.
[8] *Ibid.,* p. 15.
[9] *Ibid.,* p. 9.
[10] *Ibid.*
[11] *Ibid.,* pp. 9, 10.
[12] *Ibid.,* p. 11.

[13] *Ibid.*, p. 12.
[14] *Ibid.*, p. 13.
[15] *Ibid.*, p. 14.
[16] *Ibid.*, p. 15.
[17] *Ibid.*, pp. 15, 16.
[18] *Ibid.*, p. 16.
[19] *Ibid.*, p. 17.
[20] *Ibid.*, p. 15.

CHAPTER 4

Conversation With a Painter

1893: BATTLE CREEK, MICHIGAN

EDSON WHITE DISCOVERS THE CHARGE OF
ELLEN G. WHITE, HIS MOTHER, TO THE ADVENTIST
CHURCH TO EVANGELIZE SOUTHERN BLACKS; HE
DEDICATES HIS LIFE TO THAT MISSION.

~

*"Whom shall I send, and who will go for us? Then said I,
Here am I; send me" (Isa. 6:8).*

"SIR, HAVE YOU HEARD about my mother's 1891
testimony concerning the Colored folk?"

"No, sorry, young man; never heard of it."

"Can't say I have, Brother Edson."

"The 1891 testimony? About Colored folk? Sounds interesting, but I don't know anything about it."

~ ~ ~

James Edson White was perplexed. His mother, Ellen G.
White, had made a stirring appeal to the General Conference
workers in 1891 about the urgent need to evangelize the recently freed Blacks in the South. It had been a searing indictment of the lackadaisical attitude of the denomination toward
Black people, and the church leaders had blanched under it.

The message was so critical, in fact, that it had been published in the form of a short tract. Now it had vanished. All traces and recollections of it seemed to have evaporated.

But Edson knew that his mother had spoken on the subject. He had attended the Bible institute earlier and had spoken to Joseph Caldwell, who had casually mentioned the address in passing. Curious, Edson questioned him concerning its contents. Caldwell knew the general thrust, and even hazily recited a few direct quotations. It was then that Edson, strangely moved, asked excitedly, "Do you have a copy of the tract?" Caldwell replied, "No; I lost it."

Now the mystery of the missing tract was gnawing at Edson. What had happened to it? Was their some sort of conspiracy to silence his mother's urgent appeal? How could everyone claim to be ignorant of an event that had occurred only two years ago? He determined fiercely to get to the bottom of it.

VITAL STATISTICS

Born: James Edson White
Birthplace: Rocky Hill, Connecticut
Date: July 28, 1849
Parents: James and Ellen White
Married: 1870, Emma MacDearmon
Died: 1928

Then one warm summer day in 1893 Edson had a casual conversation with a painter at the Review and Herald Publishing Association that cleared up the haze—about the message and about the future direction of his life. This was to be one of the most crucial conversations in the history of Seventh-day Adventism.

"Nice day today, isn't it?" Edson greeted the short, friendly looking man in overalls who was busy painting the outside of the church's publishing house.

"Oh, certainly, summertime in Battle Creek is refreshing," the painter replied, gingerly stroking his brush along the side of the building. Bright streaks of white paint glimmered in the sunlight, and the unmistakable smell of enamel wafted through the air.

"The building is looking good. The paint job in the offices is excellent," Edson complimented. The man had done a superb job.

"Thank you. God's buildings should be top-notch." The painter was grinning modestly, taking pride in his work.

"How long have you been working here?" Edson asked.

"Oh, just a couple of weeks. I've really enjoyed it. There is nothing like lending a hand to help finish God's work." The painter dipped his thick brush in the can of white paint.

"So what are you doing these days?" the painter asked Edson cheerfully.

"I've been attending the Bible institute," Edson replied. "I am very interested in working for the Black people in the South."

"Really," the painter said, pausing to regard his progress.

"Yes. There are millions of Blacks in the South searching for the light of salvation. We must be the ones to give it to them. I believe it is our duty before God."

Just then the sun was eclipsed by a group of benign clouds. A cool breeze floated idly by. The painter paused and looked at Edson. "You ought to read a tract I saw about that," he said intriguingly.

At this Edson's eyes lit up. His body moved forward, and his face creased in expectation.

"What tract?" he asked, trying to be nonchalant, but failing at it.

"Well, I think it is something your mother wrote. I found a few copies of it scattered around the floor in the room upstairs about a month ago where the International

Tract Society used to be." The painter paused, interested in Edson's mounting curiosity.

Edson couldn't believe his ears! Could it be his mother's 1891 General Conference address? Was it the tract that had apparently vanished from existence?

Too engrossed to say thank you and wild with excitement, Edson sprinted up the steps of the Review and Herald building. The wooden floorboards creaked wildly under his impatient feet. Upon reaching the top of the steps, he hurled past several doors until he found the last room on the right: the International Tract Society. He grabbed the old, frail door handle. It gave. He burst inside.

HAPPY BIRTHDAY

Edson White was born on July 28, 1849, the same month that the first issue of Present Truth *was published.*

The room was dark and musty, and it was clear that no one had entered it in a long time—at least the month since the painter had been inside. The distinct smell of paper and ink filled the air. Tracts and pamphlets were piled and scattered all over the decaying furniture and thin rug. Finding the tract would be tantamount to finding a needle in a haystack. But Edson was undaunted, and enthusiastically commenced his search.

Edson had no idea how long he was at it. He hungrily leafed through stacks of paper, cutting his fingers on the sharp edges. Every once in a while he would pause when he saw a string of words that said something about his mother or duty or Black people. But then he'd discover it wasn't the one, and toss it to his left. After a while there was a menacing tower of paper to his left, threatening to topple on him. Feverishly he started another pile.

Tract after tract, manuscript after manuscript, he searched; his bones were beginning to ache. He was also getting a headache from focusing on small words in an unlighted room for so long. He jumped up and tried to turn on the light—nothing. He went to the old white window shades, turned tan by the dust. He flung them open, and the sunlight streamed in. Then he went back at it.

His pace didn't slacken. He was possessed with a holy purpose. All alone, the grown man searched for his mother's words in a forgotten room for hours. Then he saw something that might be it. He almost fainted. It was it—this was the tract. The tiny booklet—"Our Duty to the Colored People"—was at the bottom of a massive stack of papers.

Eagerly yet tenderly Edson opened the thin booklet. It was stained by something that Edson couldn't place, but it made no difference to him. The words seemed to burn indelibly into his mind. With his hand shaking and his heart pounding, he read:

"He [Jesus] died just as much for the colored people as for the white race."[1]

"Those who have a religious experience that opens their hearts to Jesus will not cherish pride but will feel they are under obligation to God to be missionaries as was Jesus."[2]

"The Lord's eye is upon all His creatures; He loves them all, and makes no difference between white and black, except that He has a special, tender pity for those who are called to bear a greater burden than others."[3]

"The ignorant and the wise, the rich and the poor, the heathen and the slave, white or black—Jesus paid the purchase money for their souls. If they believe on Him, His cleansing blood is applied to them. The black man's name is written in the book of life beside the white man's."[4]

"Those who slight a brother because of his color are slighting Christ."[5]

"If Jesus is abiding in our hearts, we cannot despise the colored man who has the same Saviour abiding in his heart. When the unchristian prejudices are broken down, more earnest effort will be put forth to do missionary work among the colored race."[6]

"God cares no less for the souls of the African race that might be won to serve Him than He cared for Israel. He requires far more of His people than they have given Him in missionary work among the people of the South of all classes, and especially among the colored race."[7]

Emma and Edson White

Edson gasped at the clarity of the words. He became more and more excited as he felt his mother's conviction and sense of urgency. He read on:

"Sin rests upon us as a church because we have not made greater effort for the salvation of souls among the colored people."[8]

"White men and white women should be qualifying themselves to work among the colored people. There is a large work to be done in educating this ignorant and downtrodden class. We must do more unselfish missionary work than we have done in the Southern States, not picking out merely the most favorable fields. God has children among the colored people all over the land. They need to be enlightened. There are unpromising ones, it is true, but you will find similar degradation among the white people; but even among the lower classes there are souls who will embrace the truth."[9]

"God will accept many more workers from the humble walks of life if they will fully consecrate themselves to His service. Men and women should be coming up to carry the truth into all the highways and byways of life. Not all can go through a long course of education, but if they are conse-crated to God and learn of Him, many can without this do much to bless others. Thousands would be accepted if they would give themselves to God. Not all who labor in this line should depend on conference support. Let those who can do so give their time and what ability they have, let them be messengers of God's grace, their hearts throbbing in unison with Christ's great heart of love, their ears open to hear the Macedonian cry." [10]

James Edson White pored over those heaven-drenched words again and again in that obscure room in 1893. That was the turn-ing point. Edson was convinced of his lifework after that. The die had been cast. James Edson would dedicate the rest of his life to giving Southern Blacks the Seventh-day Adventist message.

BEAUTIFUL MUSIC

Edson White helped to publish three hymn books. Two hymns that he wrote the music for are included in The Church Hymnal *(nos. 230 and 235).*

In the dim light of the set-ting sun Edson pondered how God had led him thus far. He had been blessed with godly parents, two pioneers of the greatest movement the earth had ever seen. They had loved him deeply and instructed him in the ways of God. He had been dramatically delivered from fatal illness several times as a child. God had watched over him.

Then he thought of his conversion, those early years when he first gave his heart to God. He remembered the days when he worked among God's people at the Review and Herald and the Pacific Press. But he had gone astray. He had started a business in Chicago in the 1880s and lost his fever for the truth. If it weren't for the Holy Spirit's persis-tent pursuit, he would have perished in his sins, forfeiting eternal life. Fortunately, he accepted the tendered grace and experienced a complete conversion. Now he had a new lease on life.

Jesus ignited him with a noble purpose, a clarion call to the gospel ministry. There in the modest room, among its di-

Edson White and Crew

sheveled surroundings, Edson bowed solemnly in the quietude. With tears in his eyes, he covenanted to spread God's gospel to the Colored people in the South, whatever cost to himself it might be.

Following his spiritual renaissance, Edson shared the tract with his friend Will Palmer. The two had attended the same Bible institute in Battle Creek, and became insepa-rable. Palmer was like Edson, daring and adventur-ous, and had also given up a business in Chicago. Palmer

Morning Star *steamer*

shared Edson's zeal, and together the two men planned their most daring endeavor. With an eye for creativity and innova-tion, they built a boat, the *Morning Star* steamer, and lit up the South with the flame of Jesus Christ. The work was extremely dangerous, and oftentimes the two men faced certain death, but God delivered them from it every time.

Through the power of God, Edson White was directly responsible for (1) a breakthrough in the Black work; (2) the formation of the Southern Missionary Society—the self-sup-porting organizational entity for the Black work;

(3) publishing the *Gospel Herald* (the forerunner of *Message* magazine); (4) starting schools for Black children; and (5) publishing *The Southern Work*. Indirectly, his work and influence helped to facilitate the establishment of Oakwood College and the creation of the Southern Publishing Association and the Southern Union Conference.

RISKY FATHER'S BUSINESS

Edson White and Will Palmer's team suffered lynching threats, bomb threats, beatings, and shootings in order to preach the gospel in the South. Many times they barely escaped with their lives.

Significantly, thousands of African-American Seventh-day Adventists can trace their acceptance of truth to this man's effort or influence. His influence on the Black work, the Adventist Church, and society in general is immeasurable. Only eternity will reveal the true extent of James Edson White's ministry.

SUMMARY

- In March 1891 Ellen White addresses the General Conference in Battle Creek, Michigan, on the need to evangelize Southern Blacks with the Seventh-day Adventist message. Her words are largely neglected and overlooked.
- Her son James Edson finds her written message, "Our Duty," in the old Review and Herald storeroom. It changes his life and provides direction for his ministry.
- From that encounter, Edson discovers the purpose of his life and initiates one of the largest and most successful evangelistic efforts of all time.
- James Edson White ranks as one of the foremost pioneers in the establishment of the Black work in the Seventh-day Adventist Church.

LIFE LESSONS

- God works through providential conversations and events to reveal the plans He has for our lives.
- Oftentimes, one can find their destiny doing what others are reluctant to do.
- It is a Christian's duty to end oppression wherever it is found.

FURTHER READING

Graybill, Ron. *Mission to Black America*. Washington, D.C.: Review and Herald Pub. Assn., 1971.

Marshall, Norwida and Stephen Norman III, eds. *A Star Gives Light*. Decatur, Ga.: Southern Union Conference of Seventh-day Adventists, 1989.

Reynolds, Louis B. *We Have Tomorrow*. Hagerstown, Md.: Review and Herald Pub. Assn., 1984.

Schwarz, Richard. *Light Bearers*. Nampa, Idaho: Pacific Press Pub. Assn., 2000.

---

[1] E. G. White, *The Southern Work*, p. 9.

[2] *Ibid.*, p. 10.

[3] *Ibid.*, p. 12.

[4] *Ibid.*

[5] *Ibid.*, p. 13.

[6] *Ibid.*, p. 14.

[7] *Ibid.*

[8] *Ibid.*, p. 15.

[9] *Ibid.*, p. 16.

[10] *Ibid.*, pp. 16, 17.

CHAPTER 5

Light Near the River

1922: SAN FRANCISCO, CALIFORNIA

AFTER BEING STRUCK BY A CAR,
NELLIE DRUILLARD RECALLS HER PROMISE
TO ESTABLISH A HOSPITAL FOR SOUTHERN BLACKS.

~

"Vow, and pay unto the Lord your God" (Ps. 76:11).

THE TIRES SCREECHED, then a sickening thud! Nellie Druillard, an elderly woman, lay on the ground, unconscious, her body crumpled in an awkward position.

People raced from all directions to the injured woman lying helplessly on the ground. A chorus of voices shouted frantically, "Call an ambulance, quick!" Several persons knelt beside her, trying desperately to assess her condition. Everyone feared she was dying. At 78 years of age, how could she survive a vehicle hitting her?

Druillard had looked both ways. The brown car had come from nowhere. It struck her just as she was crossing a hilly street in San Francisco, California. If she was to survive, it would take a miracle.

In about 10 minutes the ambulance arrived, and Nellie

Druillard was placed delicately on a stretcher and hurried to the hospital. For hours the doctors worked on her while she lay unconscious in the hospital bed. While still in intensive care, in her hospital bed, Nellie Druillard remembered, with striking clarity, a conversation that had taken place nearly 15 years before.

"The work is making wonderful progress, isn't it, Sister White?" Nellie Druillard asked as the two sat in Druillard's modest home in Berrien Springs, Michigan. They were old, dear friends, having helped spread the gospel of Jesus Christ all over the world. Both were seasoned pioneers, tempered by years of hard yet rewarding service.

"Yes, it is, Nell," Ellen White replied affectionately. "God has ever blessed our efforts. Yet more work must be done for the recently emancipated slaves." Ellen White had come to Emmanuel Missionary College for a series of official church meetings, and the two were catching up on news of the progress of God's cause.

Nellie Druilliard

"Yes, that's right. I feel the same way. But what can be done? The prejudice against anyone trying to help them seems so strong," Nellie Druillard commented. She leaned forward, a concerned look in her eyes. Although 63, she was spry and vigorous.

"The Colored people come from God's hand just like us. We owe it to them to tell them of the gospel, especially after what our race has done to them. We will encounter prejudice, so we must work intelligently and tactfully, but we must work for them nevertheless. We've missed this point as a denomination," Ellen White replied. She clenched her fist with determination. Her son Edson had been hazarding his life in the South for nearly 10 years to reach Black people. But he still seemed mostly alone in his efforts.

Nellie Druillard looked pensive. The Spirit of God was moving on her. Years of working in His vineyard had taught her to know when He was telling her to do something. But what could she do?

Sister White continued, leaning forward in her chair and choosing her words carefully. "Nell, I think God is calling you to do a special work among the Colored folk. He blessed your and your husband's efforts immensely in Africa; now He wants you to use all your talents to help Black people here in America."

Nellie nodded her head in agreement, the wrinkles on her face a testament to her wisdom and years in God's service.

"You can endure hardness, and have been crucial in the building up of God's work," Ellen White said, her words gaining momentum. "He is calling you to do more. Your work is not finished quite yet. God wants you to do one final task."

Nellie Druillard's interest was piqued. What was this final task? God had indeed blessed her with money: just recently she had received a donation from Cecil Rhodes, a man who had a diamond mining operation in Africa. She and her husband had met the ambitious man while serving as missionaries in Africa, and he had given them property for their work back then. Recently the mining mogul had written her and

Cecil John Rhodes (1853-1902) was a British imperialist and business magnate who made a fortune from diamond mining and business operations in southern Africa. He served as prime minister of Cape Colony in South Africa from 1890 to 1896. The country of Rhodesia (since 1980, Zimbabwe) was named in his honor.

said that he wanted to donate money to God's cause. Was she to use the money for the Southern work?

Ellen White looked at Nellie, conviction in her eyes. "God wants you to build a sanitarium for all of His precious Colored children in the South."

Nellie was startled. She shifted in her seat. A sanitarium? How could she go about doing that with all the prejudice and outright racism that existed in the South? She was White, but if she tried to do anything worthwhile for the Colored folks, she herself would be a target. She might even face death. She was almost 65 years old. Did she have the strength and energy required?

"God will help you and strengthen you every step of the way," Ellen White said, seeming to read Druillard's mind. "He's blessed your labors time after time. Will you do this one last thing?"

Nellie Druillard realized that the conversation was providential and knew what her duty was. She was thrilled to be used by God again in such a grand undertaking.

"Yes, I will do it," she answered. "As the Lord gives me strength, I will use it to build a sanitarium for His people." She was absolutely sincere and intended to make good on the promise, but other work took up her time.

In 1904, Druillard had moved to Tennessee with fellow pioneers E. A Sutherland and P. T. Magan to establish the Madison School, just outside of Nashville. Ellen White had talked her into going to Tennessee, too, saying that if she guided her young nephew (Sutherland) in her work, God would renew her youth. He did.

Totally immersed in the work at the school, she couldn't find the time to devote herself to the establishment of a sanitarium, which would take all of her energy. Right then the fledgling school demanded everything she had. The school flourished with Druillard's help, her financial backing keeping it afloat.

Around the same time, Nellie's precious husband, Alma, died. The loss was devastating. Her beloved husband and partner in the work of God was now gone. For a while she mourned disconsolately; then, strengthened by God with divine resolve, she resumed her life. Her husband had been a savvy businessman as well as a missionary, and he had left a good amount of money for her. She would use it also in the cause of God. Druillard didn't forget her promise to Ellen White; she just planned to go about it later.

Now this. More than 15 years later. She had come to San Francisco for the General Conference session. Instead, she was lying in a hospital bed, almost dead. Nellie Druillard started to sob, hot tears rolling down her aging cheeks. She did not want to die without doing this final great work. Throughout her life she had always been careful to be sensitive to God's voice. But her time seemed almost up, and in the last years of her life she had failed her Lord. Guilt and remorse tormented her because she had not fulfilled her promise. She couldn't even think clearly for a spell; she was dominated by her accusing emotions.

DANGEROUS OCCUPATION

Witnessing hasn't always been as safe and as harmless as it is today in America. In the early days of Adventism, after the slaves had been emancipated, sharing the gospel to the recently freed Blacks was a risky business. Many pioneers faced death on numerous occasions because of their evangelistic endeavors.

While in that lonely hospital room, Druillard made another promise—this time to God. "O Lord Jesus," she prayed, "I'm sorry for neglecting to follow Your Spirit. If

You restore me so I can work again, I will build a sanitarium for Your people."

She did recover. The doctors and nurses were astounded as the 78-year-old woman gained 100 percent use of her limbs. They healed stronger and sturdier than they were before they were broken. Druillard called Sutherland to come get her and take her back to Nashville. Like Caleb, Nellie Druillard was going to do a greater work in her old age than she had done in her youth.

Nellie Druillard arrived in Nashville determined to do what God had told her to do. She began planning for a sanitarium with fervor and enthusiasm. Along with the help of a chosen few, Druillard selected and purchased a nice plot of land facing Trinity Lane, just a little north of Nashville, and laid the foundations for five buildings patterned after the Madison School.

Riverside Sanitarium

As suspected, Druillard had to cope with an onslaught of protest and racist sentiment. People from all sides seemed to be antagonistic to the work she was trying to do. She received letter after letter of protest, and was often met by incensed individuals who threatened her with bodily harm. The opposition to her plans was so aggressive that Druillard decided to change the location of her proposed sanitarium.

Druillard moved the sanitarium to another location on Young's Lane, on top of a rocky plateau. The site was perfect because it was at a bend of the Cumberland River, on a high summit with a beautiful view of the city and surrounding locations. Moreover, it was next to a Baptist seminary, a place where Druillard was sure that no racial infractions would incur. The name for the sanitarium was an obvious choice: Riverside. The year was 1927.

Once the site was chosen and construction was begun, Druillard started training workers. With characteristic enthusiasm, she chose people who were affectionate and considerate—those who would offer godly, practical care. She trained them in hydrotherapy and nursing procedures, as well as hygiene. Soon the Riverside Sanitarium was admitting patients and training nurses.

DEDICATED SISTERS

Nellie Druillard's maiden name was Rankin. She was the best known of the famous "Rankin girls" of early Adventism. There were nearly a dozen sisters altogether, and many of them did extraordinary work for the denomination. Each of them had red hair.

For almost 10 years Druillard (affectionately referred to as "Mother D") worked arduously at the sanitarium until she felt that she had completed her God-ordained task. At first the little sanitarium and school struggled, with so few patients that Druillard had to pay for the expenses of running the facility out of her own pocket. Yet she never gave up on the Riverside Sanitarium. Druillard continued to train nurses and offer medical care. She knew that if she was faithful, God would make sure that the hospital was all He wanted it to be. When she was 92 years old, Druillard offered the beloved sanitarium to the General Conference. However, God was just beginning to work through the modest medical facilities.

Riverside was watched over by Jehovah from the outset, and He never ceased to bless the hospital that came forth from an unfortunate accident in San Francisco. The sanitarium has not only treated thousands of Black people, but has

Dr. C. A. Dent   *Dr. H. E. Ford*   *Dr. J. M. Cox*

been an inspiration to many to join the medical missionary work. Riverside has been graced and steered by some of the denomination's finest leaders and doctors. Among them are Dr. Harry Ford, Ruth Frazier Stafford, Chancy Johnson, Dr. Carl Dent, Louis Ford, Dr. J. Mark Cox, and others.

Many have devoted themselves to healthful living because of the hospital's influence. Most important, scores have accepted God's final message to earth's inhabitants because of the glowing light near the river.

This all came about through the vision, drive, and integrity of a woman of God. Nellie Druillard gave all she had to the cause of God, even into her 90s. Her service is an inspiration to all, testifying that God can use anyone, anytime, despite gender, age, or circumstances, to build up His work on earth and lead souls safely into His kingdom.

SUMMARY

- In 1922, Nellie Druillard is hit by a car while attending the General Conference session in San Francisco, California. She sustains serious injuries.
- While in the hospital bed she remembers a promise she made to Ellen White to build a sanitarium for Southern Blacks.

CM=3

- She promises God that if He restores her, she will fulfill her promise.
- God does restore her, and she goes north to establish Riverside Sanitarium in Nashville, Tennessee.

LIFE LESSONS

- God providentially uses accidents to bring about His perfect purposes.
- Even though we may not carry out our promise immediately, God will bring it to our minds and enable us to fulfill it through His power.
- God has a grand work for each to do—we just have to do it.
- God uses those who are willing, despite gender, age, disability, or race.

FURTHER READING

Graybill, Ronald. *E. G. White and Church Race Relations.* Washington, D.C.: Review and Herald Pub. Assn., 1970.

Maxwell, Mervyn. *Tell It to the World.* Mountain View, Calif.: Pacific Press Pub. Assn., 1977.

Reynolds, Louis. *We Have Tomorrow.* Hagerstown, Md.: Review and Herald Pub. Assn., 1984.

Schwarz, Richard. *Light Bearers to the Remnant.* Mountain View, Calif.: Pacific Press Pub. Assn., 1979.

Seventh-day Adventist Encyclopedia. Washington, D.C.: Review and Herald Pub. Assn., 1976.

CHAPTER 6

Under the Tent

1878: RENO, NEVADA

CHARLES KINNEY HEARS THE ADVENTIST MESSAGE
UNDER A TENT AND GOES ON TO PROCLAIM
IT TO HIS PEOPLE AROUND THE NATION.

~

"Thy words were found, and I did eat them;
and thy word was unto me the joy
and rejoicing of mine heart" (Jer. 15:16).

EXHAUSTED, CHARLES KINNEY trudged home after another backbreaking day of work. His clothes were soiled with dust, and sweat dampened them. The sun was exiting the sky and could barely be seen above the desert mountains. The broad expanse of firmament was a fantastic kaleidoscope of pastel colors creating a magnificent sight to behold. The cool dusk air was refreshing after hours of the sun's pounding rays.

The young man trudged the dusty path he traveled daily to his humble house near the end of town. Pleasant thoughts of getting home and resting his tired bones caused Charles to break out into a smile. He was on his last leg of the day—he would be in his bed in a matter of minutes.

Then as Charles rounded a bend, a tiny cluster of lights

in the distance caught his attention. The lights surrounded a dark shape. Curious, he walked toward the mysterious sight. As he got closer Charles could make out a tent with people inside. The scene was intriguing. Scores of people sat entranced, looking up front at something that Charles couldn't see yet.

Charles neared the rear of the tent, staying a comfortable distance from the still-unknown gathering. Then he saw what everyone was staring at. A thin, short man in a black suit was standing in the pulpit up front, preaching his heart out. Earnest and passionate, the speaker exhorted those present to turn their lives over to the Lord Jesus and to live the truths found in the Bible. Charles was intrigued, and wanted to hear more. He forgot about his hard day at work, his dirty clothes, and even his color. Walking straight into the tent, he sat down in the first open seat he could locate.

VITAL STATISTICS

Born: 1855
Place: Richmond, Virginia
Baptized: 1878
Wife: Shirley Hodnet
Education: Enrolled in Healdsburg College in 1883
Died: 1951

The preacher's name was John Loughborough, a Seventh-day Adventist pioneer evangelist. What Charles saw and heard that warm evening would never leave his mind. He listened as Loughborough, filled with conviction, eloquently uplifted Jesus Christ. His powerful words thrilled Charles; he was entranced, locked in his seat, his mind riveted on the words of the evangelist. His usually stern expression softened as his heart was touched by the presentation. The message matched the need of his heart. He had been waiting to hear this all of his life.

Charles Kinney had been born a slave in Richmond,

Virginia, in 1855. His early life had been marked by poverty and humiliation. He had had very few comforts, possessed next to nothing, and engaged in brutal labor every day under the blazing sun. This sparse existence had tempered him and made him painfully sober and disciplined.

Charles was 10 years old at the end of the Civil War. Now free, the young boy decided he had to get away from the South. He did not treasure the scenes of his former enslavement; furthermore, he felt an irresistible call to go west. Maybe there he could carve out a decent existence for himself.

Charles joined a group traveling west. Travel in those days was difficult and exhausting. He had to work at menial jobs along the way to earn a pittance just so he could eat two square meals a day.

After scores of stops along the way, Charles finally decided to stay in Reno, Nevada, and make his home there. It wasn't difficult to find odd jobs there, and Kinney obtained a modest place to

J. N. Loughborough

board and eventually saved up a respectable sum of money.

And now Kinney was hearing words and concepts that electrified him.

Although he was one of a few Blacks in the congregation, what he heard seemed to speak directly to him. Kinney knew about Jesus, but he had never seen Him from this angle before.

Jesus came to the earth and chose to be in an almost identical situation as that of the recently emancipated former slaves, faced suddenly with the prospect of supporting themselves with no money, education, or jobs. Jesus toiled for a living. Jesus had a humble earthly parentage. He was not a child of privilege. He was rejected in His own country. He was treated unjustly and suffered abuse. As they learned more about their Savior, Blacks in America felt a kinship with Jesus in their suffering.

As Charles thought on the love of Jesus, who came to save everyone, including people of color, he felt drawn to the Savior. While on earth, Jesus associated with those who were low on the social level. He said that His mission was "to preach the gospel to the poor," to "heal the brokenhearted, to preach deliverance to the captives, and recovering of sight to the blind, to set at liberty them that are bruised, to preach the acceptable year of the Lord." Charles saw in Jesus a friend, one who could identify with his situation.

GROW UP

Charles Kinney lived a long fruitful 96 years. During his lifetime he witnessed the African-American Seventh-day Adventist membership go from 50 to more than 25,000. Much of this was the result of his tireless efforts.

The devil had attempted to destroy the slaves' self-esteem. But the truth that Charles heard about Christ restored dignity. It taught that all people were made in the image of God, that Christ died to save them, and that He has prepared a place for them in heaven. Though a Black man, he realized he was extremely valuable in God's sight.

Slavery had separated families. His people had been taken from the African continent, chained, then herded off to America. In America, in order to foster confusion and disloyalty so that rebellion would not occur, families and friends were separated and sold to different masters. Husbands and wives were forced to separate, babies were stripped from their mothers' arms, and siblings had to say goodbye to each other, often forever.

But the truth that Charles heard was that there was one big

family in heaven and earth that could never be separated by humans. Even death bowed to the family, and all who were a part of it would one day be united—never to part again.

Slavery had encouraged abuse. The gospel that Kinney heard that night spoke of a tender God who willed that all of His creatures prosper and be in health. The speaker told of a God who shielded His creatures from harm and promised retribution where abuse was perpetrated. This God had provided a healthy lifestyle for His sons and daughters so that they could live a quality existence.

Slavery sought to rid humanity of all worthwhile values and principles. The truth restored these to their rightful place. Principles that would lead to happiness and provide an eternal barrier against sin were taught under that tent.

Slavery bred a hateful revenge in the hearts of the ones who had been wronged. The sanctuary truth taught that all wrongs would be righted through the blood of Jesus Christ. God would not palliate or excuse evil. One day all would have to reckon with His righteous judgment.

Slavery instituted a never-ending scene of toil and conflict. The slaves had to work every day. The Bible spoke of a rest for God's people called the Sabbath. Once a week God called His creatures aside and identified with their exhaustion.

Slavery ridiculed the faith in God that the slaves possessed. The gospel taught that when people ridicule you, you are blessed and will be rewarded by God. All the righteous saints of old underwent the same thing.

Slavery bred distrust in God: an attitude that questioned, "Where are You, God?" The gospel taught that God is still active in the earth and is intensely interested in the affairs of humanity. In fact, He has maintained a Spirit of Prophecy, and His voice could still be heard among His people.

Slavery fostered spiritualism. The gospel proclaimed that night taught that there would be a resurrection of the dead. All who died believing in the Savior from slavery would live again. Forever. Guaranteed.

Slavery cultivated hopelessness. Many of Kinney's brothers and sisters went down to their graves in absolute despair. But God's Seventh-day Adventist truth taught that one day the All-powerful One, Jesus Christ, would appear in the clouds with everlasting strength and glory and put down all human rule and deliver His oppressed people.

Charles Kinney couldn't believe his ears. He left the gathering with a fire burning in his soul, its warm embers warming him all night as he lay in bed thinking about what

C. M. Kinney

he had heard. Everything became new to the young man from that day on. And Kinney continued to go back to the tent at the edge of town. Night after night he sat enraptured by the voice of Jesus through John Loughborough. When a call for baptism was made, Kinney rose from his seat. The water rippled as he went down into the water and came up a new man—free indeed!

From that moment on, the forces of evil suffered a terrible loss. Kinney was as a man possessed. He was a scythe in, the hand of God, tirelessly presenting the Seventh-day Adventist message to his brother and sisters.

Charles Kinney was the first African-American to be ordained in the Seventh-day Adventist Church. He was known as a man who could bear fruit where no one else could. Constantly the conference officials put him in hardened areas where people were loath to accept the gospel.

Every time, Kinney would come through, converting scores of souls.

Kinney served God's church in every way possible. He held evangelistic meetings, preaching night after night to large numbers in tents across the nation. He colporteured from town to town, going to doors with the new truth-filled literature fresh off the press. He wrote about Seventh-day Adventist truth; his work has been published in church periodicals and books. The inspirational preacher pastored in many different places, sustaining the souls of saints and raising up new churches. He also served as a church administrator. Charles Kinney was a thought leader and mentor of the Black work, giving direction and guidance to the ever-growing Black church.

Charles Kinney's life displays the power of God in a vivid, strik-

INNOVATOR

The idea of Black conferences did not originate in the 1930s. Charles Kinney suggested the concept way back in 1889 as a means to forward the work of God and alleviate the tension between White and Black Seventh-day Adventists.

ing fashion. God guided to the West a former slave while he was still young, then led him to a place where His last-day message was being presented. The Lord aligned the truth with Charles's mind, bringing it home with surprising clarity to the young man. From there, God used Kinney's personality, drive, and determination to raise up congregations of African-American Seventh-day Adventists all over the nation. With God's power he could not be stopped. When Kinney was baptized, there were less than 50 Black Seventh-day Adventists. When he died at the age of 96, there were more than 25,000.

SUMMARY

• Charles Kinney moves west after the slaves are emancipated.

- He hears the Seventh-day Adventist message in Reno, Nevada.
- The Seventh-day Adventist message is completely relevant and directly speaks to the situation of the former slaves.
- Kinney accepts the SDA message wholeheartedly and spends the rest of his long life sharing it, playing an instrumental role in the explosive growth of the church.

LIFE LESSONS

- God frees us from bondage and equips us to spread His message.
- Truth is always relevant to our current situation, perfectly suited to our situation.
- There is no limit to the usefulness of one who accepts the truth wholeheartedly and lives to proclaim it.

FURTHER READING

Dudley, Charles. *"Thou Who Hast Brought Us."* Brushton, N. Y.: Teach Services, Inc., 1997.

Marshall, Norwida and Steven Norman III, eds. *A Star Gives Light.* Decatur, Ga.: Southern Union Conference of Seventh-day Adventists, 1989.

Reynolds, Louis. *We Have Tomorrow.* Hagerstown, Md.: Review and Herald Pub. Assn., 1984

Schwarz, Richard. *Light Bearers to the Remnant.* Mountain View, Calif.: Pacific Press Pub. Assn., 1979.

Seventh-day Adventist Encyclopedia. Washington, D.C.: Review and Herald Pub. Assn., 1976.

Spalding, Arthur. *Origin and History of Seventh-day Adventists.* Washington, D.C.: Review and Herald Pub. Assn., 1962. Vol. 1.

CHAPTER 7

The Man Who Wouldn't Stop Preaching

1886: EDGEFIELD JUNCTION, TENNESSEE

HARRY LOWE IS CONVERTED AND IS INSTRUMENTAL IN
STARTING THE FIRST BLACK SEVENTH-DAY ADVENTIST CHURCH.

~

*"We cannot but speak the things which
we have seen and heard" (Acts 4:20).*

THE HOT SUN beamed down furiously on the tiny
Tennessee town just miles outside of Nashville, Tennessee.
Even in the shade of the small shops and house roofs there
was no respite from the incessant summer heat. The smell of
grass and fertilizer hung in the shimmering air.

Harry Lowe walked slowly down the street, his collar limp
from sweat. He was out to purchase some groceries at the local
store. Just as he was about to enter, he spotted a group of Black
people milling about. They were fanning themselves under a
storefront while engaging in casual conversation. Others who
passed the group uttered a kind word or gave a courteous nod.
Lowe was familiar with them, but had never had a chance to
really witness to them. Now was his chance.

"Good day," Lowe said cheerfully as he approached the

group. Everyone stopped talking and looked at the man, dressed neatly despite the heat in a shirt, tie, slacks, and polished black shoes. *Who,* they thought, *is so bold as to approach eight strangers by himself?*

"Good day," they responded, smiling. As he came closer, they recognized the man. He was a Baptist preacher they'd seen around.

Lowe bowed slightly and introduced himself. "I'm Pastor Harry Lowe." Then he inquired about the weather and how it was affecting the crops. Most folks in that area grew a garden to feed themselves and supplement their income, so it was a good topic to break the ice.

VITAL STATISTICS

Born: *Unknown*
Birthplace: *Tennessee*
Parents: *Unknown*
Date of Baptism: *circa 1871*
SDA Ministerial License
    Granted: *1881*
Died: *1908*

"It's been mighty dry for a spell, Pastor. We certainly could use some rain soon." Several heads nodded in agreement. Every once in a while someone would take out a handkerchief and take a swipe at his face.

Harry Lowe continued the casual conversation, but inside he was observing the group and listening intently for the voice of the Holy Spirit. He wanted to direct the minds of these precious individuals to spiritual matters and was looking for a way to do it tactfully and tastefully.

"God certainly is kind to provide for us, even in this hot, dry summer," Lowe commented, watching their faces carefully.

Lowe had been born into slavery and knew that most former slaves were innately spiritual. During those long, tedious days of bondage they had to rely on the Creator just to get them through. He remembered as a boy singing old

Negro spirituals as they worked in the fields, their backs aching and their mouths dry, but their spirits refreshed by the thought of a loving God.

"Yes, He most certainly is." Several of them responded emphatically.

A young couple passed by on the sidewalk arm in arm. The group stopped talking until the couple were out of earshot. Then Lowe spoke again.

"God's been blessing me wonderfully," he said.

"He sure has blessed me too," a man said, smiling.

"He has taught me new things that have changed my life," Lowe continued. Now he had their interest. It was normal to speak of the goodness of God, but he seemed to have something further on his mind.

"What's that?" a woman asked, fanning herself profusely.

Lowe smiled. "Did you know that God gave us a day of rest?" Lowe's face beamed with happiness and contentment. "He knows how hard life is for us, so He told us in His Holy Word that we are to take a whole day off."

Lowe searched the curious expressions on each face. He hoped that what he was telling them would affect them as it had him.

"Really, a day of rest—in the Bible? Which day is that?" one man inquired.

"The Bible says that after God created the world, He rested on the seventh day," Lowe said, remembering to keep a humble tone of voice so that it wouldn't seem as though he was trying to teach them.

Some nodded their heads in agreement. They had heard something like that before. Some of them had even read it before.

"He wants us to copy Him and rest as He did," Lowe

said, unable to contain his excitement, his words bursting out like cold water from a well pump.

"Yes," one man piped up, catching on. "That's why we don't have to work Sundays—so we can go to church." Everyone related immediately to the man's declaration and shook their heads.

"Exactly," Lowe agreed. "But Sunday wasn't the day God blessed. When He rested on the seventh day, He put a blessing on that day. Sunday doesn't contain that blessing. And nowhere in the Bible are we told to rest on or keep Sunday holy."

Some in the group looked at Lowe in surprise. Wasn't he a Baptist minister? Didn't he go to church and preach to his congregation on Sunday?

RAILROAD EVANGELISM

Pastor Elbert Lane held his Edgefield Junction meetings in a train station. The Black audience sat in a room beside the freight room while the Whites sat in the freight room and on the platform.

Lowe read what they were thinking. "I thought Sunday was the true day of worship until I heard a preacher who came to this town."

By now everyone was extremely interested in what Lowe had to say. They had turned their minds in the right direction. The blazing heat had been forgotten. Lowe saw a golden opportunity to share God's plan of salvation.

"God gave us the seventh day to rest and to remember that He created us and everything on this earth. Each week we are to stop our work from sundown Friday to sundown Saturday, just as God did, and reflect on His goodness. The Bible says that this day also celebrates our release from the bondage of slavery—and the bondage of sin.

"Christ was crucified on the cross of Calvary for each one of us. He died, or rested, before sundown Friday and lay in the tomb all Sabbath, representing a completed salvation. The apostles also worshipped and honored God on this day. The Bible says that God's true saints who follow His Word by keeping His commandments will also keep this day.

"When I heard this, I couldn't believe that I and so many others had been worshipping on the wrong day all along. But I studied it in my Bible and found it to be the truth."

The men and women were stunned. They had never heard of such a thing—and moreover, an explanation given with such clarity and authority. Lowe must be telling the truth. He had preached on Sunday, and now there was a different preacher at his little Baptist church down the road. They had never heard why Lowe had stopped pastoring the church. Now they knew. What he was telling them had meant enough to him for him even to give up his job. They began questioning Lowe.

"Then why does everyone worship on Sunday?"

"Weren't the Ten Commandments done away with on the cross?"

"Does God really want us to rest on the seventh day in these modern times?"

"Won't we get fired from our jobs if we ask for the day off?"

With a prayer in his heart, Lowe masterfully fielded all of the questions that day. His shirt was wet with sweat, and at times he felt as though he was going to faint, but he couldn't stop. After 30 minutes of talking to them, he sensed that they had had enough; it was time to go.

As he turned to leave, he added, "If anyone is interested in what I have said and would like to hear the full story, I would be honored if you would stop by my house this coming Saturday. A small group of us meet each week to study the Bible."

Several promised him that they would come that week with their families; the rest said they would try to make it the next week. Lowe said goodbye and walked away, whispering a prayer for each of them.

That Sabbath Harry Lowe's humble house on the outskirts of Edgefield was crowded with people eager to hear about God and His truth. It was a happy group that met that day, with Lowe leading out. The nucleus of this group used to be a part of the Seventh-day Adventist church in the area. But because of racial tension in the Southern region, everyone agreed that it would be best for the Whites and the Blacks to worship separately until the situation died down and race relations improved.

THE FIRST BLACK SEVENTH-DAY ADVENTIST CAMP MEETING

The first Black Seventh-day Adventist camp meeting was held at Edgefield Junction, Tennessee, in 1901. This first gathering was a marked success, and the camp meeting tradition continues to this day.

The members sang and prayed and testified joyfully. Worshipping on the Sabbath was new to several, but it was clear that the Holy Spirit was there and that true worship was occurring. Soon Harry Lowe, the leader of the gathering, rose to preach.

"Greetings on this beautiful Sabbath, Brothers and Sisters. God is truly good. I see several new faces among us, and this testifies to the fact that He is still impressing people with truth and is gathering a people who will make up His last-day remnant. Terrible events are soon to break upon this earth, and we must be hid in Christ on the day of wrath. Even now Christ is preparing us to stand in the great day of His coming."

Lowe went on to preach about that great day and the events that were to precede it. The man spoke with an authority and power that could only come from believing the truth and living it. Everyone present was impressed with the solemnity of the discourse and the urgency with which Lowe presented it. This type of preaching was new and refreshing to many of them. At the close of the sermon, Lowe made an appeal. Several in the house-church dedicated themselves to Christ and His end-time message.

The small congregation that met in Harry Lowe's house was the first African-American Seventh-day Adventist church in the South, located in Edgefield Junction, Tennessee. And Harry Lowe was the first African-American pastor in the denomination.

Who was this man named Harry Lowe? Harry Lowe was born a slave in the South, probably Tennessee. Early on, his parents instilled a love for God and truth in him that was never erased, despite the circumstances of his birth. In the mid-1860s the young former slave was ordained a Baptist minister, and he told everyone he could about Jesus Christ. His ministry was successful, and he was held in high esteem by the burgeoning denomination. Lowe was constantly witnessing, always telling somebody about the God who had done so much for him. He was a tireless worker for Jesus, with immeasurable energy.

One day Lowe obtained a copy of *Signs of the Times*. An avid Bible student, he immediately recognized the articles he read as faithful to the Bible's message. He soaked up the Scripture-saturated articles and considered becoming a Seventh-day Adventist. But he knew that in order to do so he would have to leave the Baptist Church and give up all he had worked so hard to build up: his congregation, his standing, his credentials—everything.

Lowe was living in the Nashville, Tennessee, area at that time and one day had the chance to hear an Adventist preacher by the name of Elbert Lane, whose meetings he had read about in an Adventist publication. Lane was to hold meetings in a railroad station in Edgefield. This was a golden opportunity for Lowe to actually hear a person explain the truths that he had learned about solely through studying by himself.

Lowe was indeed impressed. Lane preached the uncut truth and didn't try to shore it up with rosy platitudes. Lane spoke of Jesus Christ, who loved all people, yet would in no wise countenance or palliate evil. The world was being judged, and afterward He would come to earth to gather all who had accepted His sacrifice. Those who persisted in evil could not be saved.

EARLY CONGREGATION

The second African-American Seventh-day Adventist church was organized in Louisville, Kentucky, in 1890 by Alonzo Barry. This church was later pastored by Charles Kinney.

A lot of what Lowe heard conflicted with his Puritan belief system. Yet upon further study, he found Lane's utterances in accord with the Bible. Simultaneously, Lowe could not mistake the Holy Spirit's voice—what he heard was indeed the truth of God. The Holy Spirit worked through the magazine and Lane's preaching, and Harry Lowe became a baptized Seventh-day Adventist member in the early 1880s.

The congregation that Lowe joined was the first Seventh-day Adventist church in the South. It had been raised up mainly by Lane's efforts, and now the small group was stable and steadfast. The congregation, in line with the practice of the day, had a separate seating section for Blacks and Whites. But because of mounting tensions in the

South, the group would soon split up, and a separate group of Black Adventist churches would be organized.

Harry Lowe began sharing his new faith immediately. He only regretted not having accepted it sooner. He suffered hateful persecution from his old church. They shut their doors against him and forbid him to enter their premises. They also revoked his preaching license, which could have crushed a weaker man. But not Lowe, for he knew that he was first licensed by God. He began to preach more than he ever had before.

At first there were few visible results of Lowe's witnessing. In fact, it was two and a half years before anyone joined the church through his preaching. But the Holy Spirit attended his efforts, and soon souls began to flow in. In 1886 the first Black church was formed under the leadership of Harry Lowe. Lowe was probably the first Black American Seventh-day Adventist minister.

Harry Lowe's life is a standing testimony to the power of God's truth to cut through every human imposition and overcome all odds. Harry Lowe was a survivor of the unspeakable horrors of slavery, he left a congregation that he had spent years building up and establishing a reputation in, and then he became a minister of an unpopular denomination. Even as an Adventist he faced hardships; for years he did not see any fruit or any sign that he had made the right decision. But Lowe pressed on, and now he has a place as a pioneer in the greatest movement on earth. Now there are thousands of Black Seventh-day Adventists in the South, but it all started with a man who couldn't stop preaching.

SUMMARY

- Harry Lowe becomes the first Black Seventh-day

Adventist convert in the South after hearing the preaching of Albert Lane.

- Lowe goes on to help found the first Black Seventh-day Adventist church, in Edgefield Junction, Tennessee, and become the first Black Seventh-day Adventist pastor.

LIFE LESSONS

- When one learns the truth, they are to follow it with their whole heart, despite the consequences.
- God will ultimately bless the person who does this and will multiply their efforts.
- Beginnings may be humble, but the outcome of serving God will always yield huge results in the end.

FURTHER READING

Dudley, Charles. *Thou Who Hast Brought Us Thus Far on Our Way*. Mansfield, Ohio: Bookmasters, Inc., 2000.

Reynolds, Louis. *We Have Tomorrow*. Hagerstown, Md.: Review and Herald Pub. Assn., 1984.

Spalding, Arthur. *Origin and History of Seventh-day Adventists*. Washington, D.C.: Review and Herald Pub. Assn., 1962. Vol. 1.

CHAPTER 8

Sixty-five Oak Trees
1895: HUNTSVILLE, ALABAMA

OAKWOOD COLLEGE, THE FIRST BLACK SCHOOL FOR
HIGHER LEARNING, IS ESTABLISHED IN 1896.

~

*"Though thy beginning was small, yet thy latter end
should greatly increase" (Job 8:7).*

THE THREE MEN stepped onto the land.

The Alabama landscape was sloping and uneven, undulating like a robust sea creature. Sixty-five stately, towering oak trees stood like stalwart guardians of the property. The red clay was as hard as granite. Dense brush circled the property.

The farm was not in good shape. The limbs of the trees were sagging, weeping from neglect, and derelict brush lay strewn all over. The soil had for many long years yielded cotton; now it was barren from having been so overworked. The old well was in disrepair. The buildings on the land—an old mansion house and nine slave cabins—were in a dilapidated condition. They looked like no one had entered them since the emancipation of the slaves in the mid-1860s. No, the plantation didn't look promising at all.

PROPHETIC ENDORSEMENT

Ellen White wrote some of her strongest statements about God's providential guiding of the Oakwood School. Here are some well-known excerpts: "It was God's purpose that the school should be placed here [near Huntsville]."[1] "He [God] has bestowed on the colored race some of the best and highest talents. . . . You have precious opportunities here [at Oakwood]."[2] "It was the providence of God that the Huntsville School farm was purchased."[3] "Instruction was given me that this farm must not be sold."[4]

The property had a dark history. The 360-acre site was the former home of slave owners and hundreds of slaves. James Beasley and his family, the former plantation owners, were reported to have severely whipped their slaves for no apparent reason before the workday started. Those who passed the plantation could hear thunderous cracking of whips and plaintive wails from the unfortunate slaves. Meanwhile, the surrounding Madison County was the home of degrading and dehumanizing acts. Mutilation and lynchings were reported to have taken place nearby.

The three men at the gate—O. A. Olsen, president of the General Conference; G. A. Irwin, director of the Southern District; and Harmon Lindsay, a former General Conference employee—had been sent by the General Conference Committee to purchase land for a school for Black young people in the South. They were convinced that this was the land that God would have them purchase.

Because of the diligent effort of many individuals, it was necessary to establish a separate school for Blacks. James Edson White and his team had faithfully carried out their work in the South against tremendous odds. Financial backing was always hard to come by. Denominational support was also lacking. Materials and transportation were always scarce. And they hazarded their lives on innumerable occasions.

They had been threatened with death by infuriated mobs. Some of White's team had been whipped and beaten. Some had to flee the South for fear of their lives. But despite all of this, White reached a large group of Blacks in the South with the gospel.

White's evangelism included not only the presentation of the gospel but basic education. A school was conducted on the *Morning Star*. However, it soon became clear that this would not be enough. A permanent location would provide the further schooling opportunities that were needed. The Black converts needed a place where they could obtain a broader education—not only to support themselves, but to be equipped to help finish God's work on the earth.

So these high-ranking men in the denomination, with

OAKWOOD FIRSTS

Students: *November 16, 1896*
Graduation: *1909 (Nursing)*
1912 (Ministerial)
Principal: *Solon M. Jacobs*
Constructed Building: *November 16, 1896, boys' dorm and classrooms*
Black President: *J. L. Moran, 1932*
Professor with a Ph.D.: *Eva Dykes, 1944*
Accreditation: *December 4, 1958*

the prodding of Ellen White and her son, had set out to establish a school for Black people. The three men went to Alabama, a state that was central to the Black work, to select the property, with a budget of only $8,000. The unpromising land the men visited that historic day was the Beasley estate, which comprised some 360 acres. The church officials were optimistic: the land was in bad shape, but with diligent effort it could be made into a thriving farm. They took a favorable recommendation of the land back to the General Conference Committee in Washington, D.C., and the church purchased it in 1895.

J. J. Mitchell came from California to help start up the school as its first manager. Mitchell was selected because he was an excellent farmer—it was said that he could turn bones into human beings. One summer night he and O. A. Olsen went to take a look at the land. What Mitchell saw totally crushed his spirit.

"This is the land?" Mitchell gasped. He surveyed the property that the church had just purchased and commissioned him to oversee. All he saw was destitution and abandonment.

"Yes, it looks unpromising, but with—" Olsen was interrupted by a desperate Mitchell.

"I will not be the manager of this! It is hopeless! I don't see how . . ." Mitchell walked off into the black night, tossing his hands in the air in despair. He resigned as manager subsequently.

But later when Ellen White saw the land, she

WHAT'S YOUR NAME?

The Oakwood School has had many names in its 100-plus years of existence:
Oakwood Industrial School (1896)
Oakwood Manual Training School (1904)
Oakwood Junior College (1917)
Oakwood College (1943)

was enthusiastic. She saw more than what human eyes saw; she glimpsed the rugged plot through divine eyes. Impressed by God that the property was divinely ordained by God to fulfill a special role in the spreading of the gospel and the work of the last days, Ellen White urged the brethren to buy the land without delay. She would later say that the school that was to be built on the land was to be a powerful tool in the hands of God and that young people who graduated from its halls would proceed to give God's last message of mercy to all parts of the globe. She could not say enough about the school and its potential.

So the Beasley estate was purchased by the General

Conference in 1895. The name that the land was to be given was obvious—Oakwood, after the 65 towering trees that graced the land. Soon General Conference personnel, wearing overalls, showed up and began laboring in its fields. Many Adventist officials had their hand in the building of this "unpromising school" in Alabama. Other fieldworkers were hired to work the land, and later students came to lend a hand.

The first order of the day was, of course, water. Huntsville, Alabama, was a huge resource for water because of the "big spring" in the heart of the small town. The spring produced upwards of 24 million gallons of pure water daily. But the challenge was getting the water to the Oakwood property. The wells on the land itself proved

The Oakwood Farm

to be ineffectual and ran dry after a few hours of priming. The innovative pioneers tried a couple of systems to procure water that failed: windmills, manual hauling, digging, etc. Finally the hard work paid off, and they established a reliable irrigation system.

Much time and labor were spent in actually clearing the land. Weeds and foliage dominated the landscape. Then the soil had to be cultivated and worked so that the future students would indeed be able to learn soil culture and be able to reap financial benefits from crops. And of course, the buildings had to be renovated and made functional and presentable. The job seemed impossible, but the staff on a whole was indomitable and loved the challenge, rising to it in the strength of God.

As with all Seventh-day Adventist work for Blacks in the South, vitriolic resistance was put forth by irate Whites. The Oakwood property was especially in a vulnerable position to these threats because they happened to come largely from their neighbors. Many in the White population in Huntsville, Alabama, and the general South feared that Blacks would overrun the area. So the Oakwood overseers and administrators sought to win their neighbors over with acts of kindness, letting them know that they were there to serve and bless, not to impose or conquer. The acts of kindness worked wonderfully, and soon most in the community were interested in helping to build up the ambitious project called Oakwood.

HUNTSVILLE NOW

Population: 159,636
Metropolitan: 355,488
Number of colleges and universities: 6
*Number of historically Black
    colleges and universities: 3*
*Number of Seventh-day Adventist
    churches: 10*
*Known for: NASA Space Center,
Redstone Arsenal, Cummings
Research Park, U.S. Space and
Rocket Center*

All the hard work paid off. The situation totally reversed itself. Now the land was promising. For the first time many began noticing the beautiful mountains surrounding the property just miles away on every side. The old buildings, once renovated, turned out to be diamonds in the rough and added bonuses to the purchase of the property. The land itself, once hard as granite, slowly began to yield crops in abundance.

It was soon discovered that the city of Huntsville was a wonderful neighbor for the young school. Huntsville was one of the most progressive Southern cities, with a population of approximately 13,000, with water springs famous around the world, and with an industrial growth rate that was legendary. Moreover, the city had stayed far away from the violent crimes known to have been committed in other parts of Madison County. Instead, Huntsville was known to be progressive and sophisticated when it came to the issue of race.

Further, a burgeoning Black school was only miles away from Oakwood in Normal, Alabama, called the State Agricultural and Mechanical College for Negroes (later called Alabama A&M University). The school and those who ran it were very kind to Oakwood and aided the fledgling school in its development.

G. A. Irwin

And so were the modest yet remarkable beginnings of the Oakwood School. The first principal appointed was Solon Jacobs, on April 3, 1896. The doors to the Oakwood School were officially opened five months later, on November 16. On that opening day 16 enthusiastic students received instruction from Oakwood's slim staff, and the students are now famously known as "the original sixteen." The original cur-

H. Lindsay

riculum consisted of a basic English course, Bible classes, a few general subjects such as history and math, and of course, industrial arts (hard labor in the fields).

It was rough on the students those first couple of years. Food was hard to come by, and it was reported that there was only one reading textbook in the whole school. The plight of the school came to the attention of some of the denominational leaders, and they began agitating to get more money for the Huntsville school. Ultimately, the students endured, and the work of God prospered gloriously.

LEADERS OF
OAKWOOD COLLEGE

Oakwood has been blessed with 10 presidents in its 109-year existence:
James I. Beardsley (1917-1923)
Joseph A. Tucker (1923-1932)
James L. Moran (1932-1945)
Frank L. Peterson (1945-1954)
Garland J. Millet (1954-1963)
Addison V. Pinkney (1963-1966)
Frank W. Hale, Jr. (1966-1971)
Calvin B. Rock (1971-1985)
Benjamin F. Reaves (1985-1996)
Delbert W. Baker (1996-present)

Buildings went up rapidly. The old slave mansion was dug up and renovated, turning out to be a diamond in the rough. In 1899 a study hall three stories high was erected by Oakwood students. Oaklawn, the principal's quarters, was completed in 1906. Butler Hall was open for classes in 1908, and East Hall, the sanitarium building, was finished in 1909. A dwelling house for orphans was built in 1912. During World War I an apartment building for faculty members and a boys' dormitory were built. Industrial buildings were also erected: the trademark barn and silos that still stand today, a garage, a printshop, and a laundry building were all constructed in the first decade of the twentieth century. By 1916 the school had an impressive 22 buildings on its property.

Under varied leadership, the curriculum of Oakwood Industrial School expanded from the trinity of English, Bible, and Industrial Arts to almost every branch of knowledge, including such specialized subjects as astronomy,

J. L. Moran, First Black President of Oakwood

anatomy and physiology, botany, psychology, rhetoric, nursing, organ, history, and voice. Through able leadership and God's guidance, the school continued to grow and expand in all aspects, becoming a marvel to the community and the world.

The Oakwood School went through various name changes and leaders. Students came and went, leaving the institution ordained by God to serve the world. Leaders carried the school through dynamic vision, strength of will, and charismatic personalities. The school developed a worldwide reputation as it eventually took its place among the prestigious schools of the denomination and nation. But through it all, the Lord had His hand on the Oakwood School and guided it in His providence.

THEN . . . NOW

Category	1896	2003
Enrollment:	16	1,787
Countries Represented:	1	45
Male/Female Ratio	7/8	765/1,018
Majors/Subjects	3	90
Graduates:	0	251
Number of Buildings:	2	60
Number of Teachers:	3	175

In a way, Oakwood College's history is a microcosm of the Black Seventh-day Adventist work. It began in earnest by a divine act of God in which He freed the slaves on His own initiative. Then He gave visions to His chosen prophetess, and she faithfully related them to a rather lackadaisical church in regard to the Black work. But her son James Edson White picked up on it through a "coincidental" conversation with a painter. From then on, through indomitable will and sheer force of character, he hazarded his life to share the message that meant so much to him with the Black residents of the South. His work was successful because it was God's own cause. Blacks were educated, and from there a school was formed through God's special guidance.

The Oakwood Industrial School faced some rocky years. Finances were always short. At times the denomination's backing was weak. Student enrollment was low, dipping to scary depths at times. The institution faced naysayers and persecutors. But it was God's school, not man's, and God personally saw to it that Oakwood prospered and marched forward.

As a result, Oakwood College (which is now 109 years old) has sent out thousands of graduates from all countries and backgrounds. These graduates have gone on to serve humanity in almost every capacity and have turned every part of the globe upside down with God's Seventh-day Adventist message. The school has contributed immeasurably, not only to God's work, but also to the uplifting of humanity as a whole. The rocky, red soil has yielded fruit that only eternity can measure.

Oakwood College was cited in U.S. News and World Report *as one of the best colleges in the Southern region for the past five years.*

SUMMARY

- Three General Conference representatives decide that an obscure piece of property in Huntsville, Alabama, should be the site of the first Black Seventh-day Adventist institution of higher learning.
- Ellen White confirms that decision through her enthusiastic encouragement.
- The school opens in 1896 and becomes a premier General Conference institution, training thousands of young people from all over the world.

LIFE LESSONS

- What at first seems impossible and without promise can become phenomenal and world-renowned through the power of God.

• Greatness comes only from perseverance through setbacks and obstacles.

FURTHER READING

Baker, Delbert. *Telling the Story*. Loma Linda, Calif.: Loma Linda University Printing Services, 1996.

Oakwood College Fact Book 2002-2003. Huntsville, Ala.: Office of Institutional Effectiveness. Oakwood College.

Reynolds, Louis. *We Have Tomorrow*. Hagerstown, Md.: Review and Herald Pub. Assn., 1984.

Sepulveda, Ciro, ed. *The Ladies of Oakwood*. Huntsville, Ala.: Oakwood College Press, 2003.

Simpson, Fred. *The Sins of Madison County*. Huntsville, Ala: Triangle Publishing Co., 2000.

Spalding, Arthur. *Origin and History of Seventh-day Adventists*. Washington, D.C.: Review and Herald Pub. Assn., 1962. Vol. 2.

Warren, Mervyn. *Oakwood! A Vision Splendid*. Collegedale, Tenn: College Press, 1996.

---

[1] Speech at Oakwood on June 21, 1904, in E. G. White, *Manuscript Releases,* Vol 6, p. 214.

[2] *Ibid,* pp. 211-214.

[3] Ellen G. White. *Last Day Events,* p. 102.

[4] *Ibid.*

CHAPTER 9

Faith, Steel, and a Revolver
1887: ELLISVILLE, MISSISSIPPI

ANNA KNIGHT BECOMES THE FIRST BLACK WOMAN OF ANY
DENOMINATION TO DO MISSIONARY WORK IN INDIA.

~

"Go ye therefore and teach all nations" (Matt. 28:19).

IT WAS SABBATH. The young woman ventured out into the frosty air, quietly weaving her way through the woods, searching for an ideal place to worship. The white snow and silver icicles hung heavily on the thick trees. Her feet crunched in the snow on the ground while the wind whipped in her face, flecks of ice landing on her. She seemed almost immune to the wintry chill—this was her holy day, and nothing would distract her from worship.

She found a nice secluded spot, hidden far from the well-worn path, about 40 yards away. The place she chose was hidden from the path by two huge oak trees that gallantly shielded the young woman. She would be safe here. The young girl gathered some pine knots in order to build a small fire. Her hands were almost frozen from carrying the cold

96

wood, but it was all worth it when the fire was crackling, producing a warm draft of air. It was here that Anna Knight prayed and sang and read from a Bible that she had picked cotton to pay for.

Every Sabbath Anna chose a different spot to worship in. Sometimes she followed the path deep into the forest, walking until she thought it best to stop. Other times she went a short way, then fishtailed through the foliage to a hidden spot. She did this because many girls who ventured into the woods—or any other place, for that matter—were sometimes violently raped. Mobs of men, White and Black, lurked in the shadows, silently stalking their prey.

Yet Anna Knight was not scared. First of all, she had Jehovah on her side, and she had a steellike faith in His power to protect her. Then also, she carried a small revolver in her dress pocket. She had warned all in the community that she would not be afraid to shoot anyone stupid enough to give her trouble. Everyone knew that she was not joking, for when her family was hungry, she would not just go out and catch a chicken by hand; she would shoot its head off with her gun!

VITAL STATISTICS

Born: *March 4, 1874*
Birthplace: *Gitano, Mississippi*
Parents: *Newton Knight and Georgianna Knight*
Date of baptism: *1893*
Marital status: *single*
Education: *Graysville Academy, Mount Vernon Academy, Battle Creek Sanitarium*
Died: *1972*

How did Anna Knight come to learn about the Sabbath truth?

Anna was born in 1874, the illegitimate child of a White father and a former Black slave—a scandal that nearly ruined both of their lives. Her origin was, of course, kept as secret as possible, and Anna went to live with her mother's family on their rented farm in the backwoods of Mississippi, in an old log cabin. As the light-skinned girl grew, she became bored and dissatisfied with her surroundings. Every day was full of the same monotony: work, work, work. The grueling labor yielded few results; Blacks were still oppressed. Moreover, Anna never met anyone new, went anywhere new, or learned anything new. Her adventurous spirit looked for some sort of action.

One day in 1891 Anna was reading a local paper in her small community. Through various means she had taught herself to read, so now she would read whenever she had time and material. But the latter was running out. There were almost no books in the house, since she was the only one living there who could read. Anna's eyes lit up when she spotted a column called Exchange, in which she could send away for some novels. This really interested her—anything to pep up her life and get her mind off the mundane.

WILD CHILD

On rainy days or Sundays Anna Knight would ride her pony and practice hitting targets with her revolver. She became an expert sharpshooter.

She sent away for some novels, lying about her color, age, and status. She was considered Black, was 16 years old, and was poor. Anna was overjoyed to find a barrage of books and magazines coming to her mailbox almost daily, it seemed. Soon she had received so much that she had a problem storing all of it. She read the material with relish, especially loving the novels' salacious and exciting tales.

But soon sandwiched in among the mail she received were publications of a totally different nature—magazines called *Review and Herald* and *Signs of the Times* and *Youth's Instructor*. These magazines were different from the shady novels she was used to seeing, and the content was different also. There were Bible texts and references to God. Anna read them diligently, impressed but not quite convinced that everything in them was correct. Her interest had been piqued, though, and she wanted a Bible of her own to see if what she was reading was true.

Anna looked and asked around for a copy of the Bible; it was tough to find one among people who were basically illiterate. But one day Anna was over-joyed when she discovered that her uncle had an old worn copy. She begged him to give it to her. He said that she could work for it by picking 200 pounds of cotton. Anna didn't think twice about the offer. Soon the precious book was hers.

Young Anna Knight

The determined young girl studied the Word of God every chance she got, comparing scripture with scripture and taking in the great truths she encountered. She was amazed to discover that everything she read in the magazines was in accord with the Bible, and she embraced each Seventh-day Adventist truth. The teenage girl who had been sending Anna the tracts worked diligently with her, and Anna de-cided to get baptized—against the wishes of her family. She was persecuted so badly that she had to leave her home and go to Chattanooga, Tennessee, nearly 400 miles away, in order to practice her newfound faith in peace.

Anna continued to face difficulties in Chattanooga, as she had before. She attended an Adventist school in Graysville, Tennessee, but because of the color of her skin she was told that she would be mobbed if she continued to attend. So Anna stayed in her room and did a sort of home-schooling program. Despite the glaring hypocrisy she encountered, Anna never wavered in the Adventist faith. Later she attended Mount Vernon Academy in Ohio.

Anna Knight went on to study at the Battle Creek Sanitarium in Michigan. Once again she worked tirelessly, this time in order to pay for her schooling. She entered the nursing program, but because of so much overwork she was too ill to finish it. She was quarantined by the school's doctor, yet she was able to sneak back to her classes. She ended up completing the program.

ON FIRE FOR CHRIST

Steps to Christ *was sent to Anna Knight with other Adventist literature. She read it in secret at night by piling fat pine knots in a corner of a barn and burning them.*

Anna's family and others back home in Mississippi begged her to come and start a school. They wanted an education like the one Anna had obtained. Anna did return to Mississippi, and started three schools and a home nursing practice despite constant death threats because of her denunciation of alcohol use and the color of her skin. She confronted these threats directly, daring anyone to touch her. And of course, on the way to school each morning she carried a Bible, *Our Little Friends*, and a revolver in her bag. She was not touched.

Dr. John Harvey Kellogg was very impressed with Anna Knight's indomitable spirit and brilliant mind, and invited her to be a delegate to the 1901 General Conference session in Battle Creek, Michigan. While there she met J. L. Shaw and his wife, who had just returned from Africa. They had received another call to go to India and were excited about it. The couple needed two trained nurses to go with them. Anna recalled that she had always wanted to serve as a missionary to the women in India. She pledged to herself that if someone took over her school in Mississippi, she would stay in India until the Lord came.

But a couple of days later Anna began to rethink her vow. Who would take charge of her school? Would they care for it and provide competent leadership? What would everyone think of her leaving her people in the South, who needed so much help, to go to India? Would they think that she had deserted them? Would she be cast off? Was it really God's will for her to go?

Anna began to cry profusely. Darkness pressed in on her, and terror filled her mind. More than anything she wanted to be in God's will. More than anything she wanted to finish His work. She fell to her knees sobbing. She prayed a desperate prayer to God in her direct manner, saying that all the people of the world were His children and that she would go

PISTOL-PACKIN' MAMA

A group of rough men formed a posse to murder Anna Knight for speaking out against the use of alcohol. As she rode through the woods on horseback, one of the hidden men yelled out, "Here comes the pistol-packin' mama!" Knight was fired at, but escaped unharmed.

wherever He bade. Then her former resolve again took hold of her, and she never shed another tear about the matter, not even when she said goodbye to her dearest friends. Jesus tendered too much strength for her to succumb to weakness.

Anna Knight left for India in 1901, taking a train to New York City; a ship to Liverpool, England; a train to London; a boat to Calais, France; a train to Paris; a train to Marseille; a boat to Port Said; and finally a boat to Bombay, India. All in all, the trip took 30 days! Anna Knight had become the first Black female missionary of any denomination to serve in India.

Anna gave her heart and soul to the work in India, serving in any way she could to help the people. Her versatility was legendary: she worked as a nurse, farmer, schoolteacher, colporteur, orphanage caretaker, and Bible instructor, doing everything from pulling teeth to planting crops.

Again and again she would faint from exhaustion and overwork, but the Spirit of God strengthened her, and she

Anna Knight

would arise each time, stronger than before. Many times her life was threatened as it was back in the old days in the South. She told of being robbed and stalked by posses of men with long sharp knives. But as before, she faced death fearlessly and came out a conqueror, serving in India for six years.

After successfully serving in India, Anna Knight returned to the United States and continued to do what she could to build up God's cause. Anna was a woman of almost superhuman abilities and possessed a spirit of iron. She lectured extensively, becoming an icon for Christian education and health promotion, renowned far and wide for her experience and expertise.

Anna Knight never stopped working throughout her long life. At 98 she served as president of the National Colored Teachers' Association. Shortly before her death she was awarded the Medallion of Merit Award for her outstanding service to Seventh-day Adventist education.

Anna Knight's life is an inspiration to all people, but especially to those who feel that life or God has dealt them a bad hand because of their circumstances. Anna Knight had many things working against her: being illegitimate, being a woman, and being a racial minority. Because of these things, she was looked down on during the time in which she was most prolific. Yet Knight never succumbed to complaining or depression. She summoned the powers of her will and relied on her God and did extraordinary things.

She is recognized as being among the first of thousands of Black Seventh-day Adventist Christian missionaries who have served their church valiantly in every part of the globe and promoted eternal principles powerfully. Through them thousands of souls have been won to God's saving message.

ONCE AN ADVENTIST, ALWAYS AN ADVENTIST?

Dr. John Harvey Kellogg displayed great confidence in Anna Knight and took her under his wing. He helped her attend Battle Creek College and was instrumental in sending her to India. She was worried about the great doctor when he strayed from the church, and visited him at his house when he was an old man He took Knight to his study, where he kept all the books that were most valuable to him. Scores of Ellen White titles sat on the shelves, worn from use.

SUMMARY

- Anna Knight discovers the Adventist message and begins a school in Mississippi.
- She is impressed to do missionary work in India and becomes the first Black woman of any denomination to do so.
- She does outstanding work there, then returns to the United States to lecture and establish schools.

LIFE LESSONS

- God uses those mightily who dedicate themselves to Him and look for ways to forward His cause.
- Circumstances are not obstacles to God—He turns

them for good.
• God needs fearless people to work for Him, those who refuse to be intimidated by circumstances.

FURTHER READING

Chilson, Adrian. *They Had a World to Win*. Hagerstown, Md.: Review and Herald Pub. Assn., 2001.

Knight, Anna. *Mississippi Girl*. Nashville, Tenn.: Southern Pub. Assn., 1952.

Sepulveda, Ciro, ed. *The Ladies of Oakwood*. Huntsville, Ala.: Oakwood College Press, 2003.

Spalding, Arthur. *Origin and History of Seventh-day Adventists*. Washington, D.C.: Review and Herald Pub. Assn., 1962. Vol. 1.

"Story of Anna Knight." As told to A. W. Spalding in Atlanta, Ga., Nov. 19, 22, 1914. Ellen G. White Estate Document File: 372-1, 1914.

CHAPTER 10

Adventism's Harlem Renaissance

1929: NEW YORK, NEW YORK

JAMES HUMPHREY AND HIS CHURCH ARE DISFELLOWSHIPPED FROM THE SEVENTH-DAY ADVENTIST CHURCH BY AN ACT OF THE GENERAL CONFERENCE IN 1930.

~

"For he supposed that his brethren would have understood how that God by his hand would deliver them: but they understood not" (Acts 7:25).

LOUIS DICKSON SQUIRMED in his chair, the ancient joints creaking under his weight. The room was reverently silent as the man shuffled words in his head. Forming and reforming sentences, he tried desperately to find the right combination. Tact was paramount—this was a delicate subject, and he was well aware of the ramifications involved.

Dickson, president of the Greater New York Conference of Seventh-day Adventists, leaned back as he considered something else. Tact, yes. But he must be firm. This must not happen in God's church. Dickson slowly began his letter:

"Dear Brother Humphrey:

"Recently information has come to me regarding a plan that you are said to be connected with in connection with some property matter in the Upstate. The report has come that you and the officers of your church are promoting this project among your members, with the object of firmly establishing a Colored colony, sanitarium, and old people's home. Of course, these are merely reports, and I must come to you for facts. Naturally, questions arise and criticisms are offered, and I am in no position to disillusion anybody's mind upon it as long as I am totally in the dark regarding the facts. I would be glad to have you drop me a line setting me right on this matter, and giving me any other information that you think will be helpful in explaining what may be going on.

"Assuring you of my sincere desire to cooperate in every good thing, with kindest regards, I remain,

"Sincerely, your brother,
"L. K. Dickson."[1]

Dickson sat back in his chair and looked at the letter contentedly. It would do. He called his secretary to mail it.

~ ~ ~

"Pastor Humphrey, you have a letter here from Elder Dickson."

Humphrey took the envelope from his secretary's hand and immediately sat down to read it, curious about its contents. He had known it would come. He opened the letter, neatly severing the envelope paper. He read it through once, then again, then put it down and pondered it.

Humphrey sighed a long, tired sigh, weary of his years of bearing the burden of this "race thing." His people needed help, badly.

James K. Humphrey was pastor of the First Harlem Seventh-day Adventist Church in New York City. He had been converted to Seventh-day Adventism through the efforts of a Black layperson named J. H. Carroll. From him Humphrey had taken hold of the gospel torch and had almost immediately met with tremendous success. Humphrey labored in different parts of New York City, raising up four congregations in a matter of a few years. He began construction of the first Black SDA church in New York City and one of the first in the North.

Humphrey was known to be an intelligent, innovative, charismatic man of God, and he rose in stature in the denomination. In 1922 he was invited to address the world church at the General Conference session and also served on several General Conference committees. He was an articulate spokesperson for Black Seventh-day Adventists, and was sought after for advice and guidance concerning his people. Without a doubt Humphrey was one of the premier pioneers of the Black Seventh-day Adventist work.

SON TO FATHER TO WORLD

When James Humphrey heard the Seventh-day Adventist truth, he didn't keep it to himself. Along with bringing hundreds to God's last-day truth, he also converted his father, a Baptist minister. His father, who pastored a church in Jamaica, went on to spread the Adventist message to the Caribbean island. His efforts are still felt today as Adventism in Jamaica is thriving.

But all was not well with the Black work. In 1920 there was only one Black school in the United States, Oakwood Junior College in northern Alabama, and Blacks were not normally admitted to other Adventist institutions of higher learning. In fact, the director of the School of Nursing in what is now Loma Linda University wrote this letter to a Black woman seeking admission:

"We do not see our way clear to accept you to the nurses'

course because of your nationality. We have had some difficulty in training students of your nationality before."

Moreover, Blacks were not even allowed in Adventist sanitariums. They could not be treated, and even Black laborers were kept out of the treatment rooms. The situation

was all the more offensive when one realized that Blacks gave tithes and offerings in support of the institutions that they could not enter.

Segregation and discrimination were the order of the day. Cafeterias, dorms, and churches were segregated: Blacks were not allowed in the White sections. Blacks held no leadership positions in the conferences; therefore, they had no real voice in the denomination. The situation was discouraging and reprehensible, and cried out for attention.

J. K. Humphrey

James Humphrey was not impervious to the situation. He urged the General Conference to treat Blacks equally. When that approach didn't work, he proposed the idea of Black conferences. He saw this as a way for Blacks to get equal treatment and for the work to prosper. He did not wish to separate from his White brethren, but the situation was grim and his people needed help, or the work among them would die out. The Black congregations he visited were becoming increasingly vocal about the unfair treatment they were receiving.

In spite of his efforts, the General Conference rejected proposals for Black conferences, feeling that the idea was premature. They wanted more time to consider the issue, to take surveys and research the feasibility of the plan. Humphrey was dissatisfied with the verdict, to put it lightly.

He saw the General Conference's response as a rejection and felt that they had a lack of knowledge and sympathy to the plight of Black Adventists. He felt that it was his duty to act, since he was one of Black Adventism's main leaders. He thought the General Conference was slow to listen and dictatorial. Other Black leaders, though reluctant to speak out, felt the same way. For too long Black leaders had sat by and done nothing while Black members were ignored and mistreated. Humphrey had plans, great plans, to raise his people to the high places that God had for them. With God's help he would ennoble his downtrodden brothers and sisters. This was the time, the place; Humphrey felt that he had a divine mandate to action.

Humphrey devised a plan for a resort known as the Utopia Health Benevolent Association. This association would thrive in a chosen spot 45 miles out of New York City, on the New Jersey shore. The resort would include a much-needed school, an orphanage, a senior citizens' home, sports facilities, swimming pools, and other facilities beneficial to the health and upbuilding of Blacks. Humphrey stated the aim of the organization in a brochure: Utopia was to "provide healthful recreation for thousands of Colored people who are interested in the care of their bodies and the betterment of their minds."

Humphrey was almost sure that if he told the conference of his plans they would be rejected and he would not be allowed to continue. So he decided to do it with the help of his church and, of course, his God. He was certain that God loved Black people as He did whites, and that He was leading and that these plans would succeed. Lots on the property would be sold to persons "of good moral standing" to help fund the project. Humphrey's members worked diligently, soliciting in the streets, passing out flyers, and signing up interested people to participate in fund-raising events.

Since Humphrey didn't share his plans with the General Conference administrators, Dickson and other church leaders found out about Humphrey's activities from rumors and gossip.

A BIG CHURCH

Because of God's mercy and James Humphrey's tireless efforts, in 1920 when the First Harlem Seventh-day Adventist Church was founded, the membership was just at 600. This accounted for a sixth of the entire Black Seventh-day Adventist membership in the United States.

Naturally, church leaders were wary of anyone who set about doing projects without the church's blessing and involvement. Divisiveness was rampant in those days, and they had no idea what Humphrey was thinking or doing. Unfortunately, communication and dialogue between the two groups were nonexistent. Suspicions were high, and opinions became rigid.

~ ~ ~

Humphrey slumped in his chair, pensive. Dickson, president of the Greater New York Conference, had written the letter Humphrey held in his hand in response to his Utopia Park plan. Humphrey was in a bind. His people needed help, but at the same time he wanted to remain in accord with the conference and God's larger body of Seventh-day Adventists. He had been a champion of Adventism and had heralded the message where no one else would go—to the slums and ghettos of New York City. Many times individuals had come to him with reports of church discrimination and pressure to leave the denomination. But Humphrey's reply was always the same: "I refuse to leave God's church."

Humphrey had deliberated on the matter for a couple of days before replying. He was tired from the whole situation, but once again drew on the never-ending reserve of energy that came from his zeal for God's work. Tired and sad over the plight of his people, Humphrey took up his pen and thoughtfully began to write:

"My dear Brother:

"Your letter of the thirteenth . . . comes to hand. I was very glad to hear from you. I understand from your letter that you were informed of a project on foot in the purchase of some property upstate by the Colored people, upon which a sanitarium and old folks' home are to be built, and in which I and some of my members are interested.

"It is true that some of us are interested in the effort to help the Colored people realize these institutions that we so sorely need."

Humphrey paused. Now he must tell the president plainly that the work he was involved in could not be interfered with because it would save souls. Nothing most prevent souls from being saved from ruin and degradation. Humphrey painfully penned the following words, trying to be as congenial and sensitive as possible.

"It is not a denomination effort, inasmuch as our people are unable to maintain one. I thank you very much for your expression of kindly interest and your desire to cooperate in this good work, but it is absolutely a problem for the Colored people."

Humphrey paused again. Should he change that last sentence? He wanted the bettering of Blacks to be the work of all people, but no one seemed interested in helping.

Humphrey hated injustice and discrimination with a passion. No one seemed to want to get rid of the malicious thing! God's people were dying! Humphrey ended the letter:

> "With best regards, I remain
> "Yours sincerely,
> "J. K. Humphrey."[2]

~ ~ ~

After the exchange of letters, events escalated in rapid succession. Neither man would shift from his position. Both were men of God, desiring to do His will, yet they could not see eye to eye.

Soon the Greater New York Conference officials met with Humphrey. The conference representatives appealed to Humphrey to rethink his plan and submit to the conference. They pointed out that he was proceeding without the backing of the church and was outside the auspices of God's ordained movement. His actions were unwise and divisive. Help, they said, would come for the Colored people, but in God's own time. They advised him to wait patiently. Humphrey replied with a kind "Thank you but no thank you." Without fanfare, long deliberations, or probing committees, Humphrey was summarily informed that he was no longer a pastor or member of the Seventh-day Adventist denomination.

The conference proceeded to meet with the members of the First Harlem church. The atmosphere was ominous and threatening, like dark, gray rain clouds creeping over the sky. Several church officials were present, including General Conference president W. A. Spicer. Dickson spoke at length on his position, trying to persuade the Harlem congregation that the conference had taken a fair, rational position.

As events unfolded, the situation heated up. The members of Humphrey's church strongly felt ignored, mistreated, and dictated to. As a result, they voiced their opinions vehemently. They felt that the conference had done them wrong by doing nothing at all for their race. The conference offered no suggestions to help, whereas their beloved Pastor Humphrey offered a plan with great promise. They supported Humphrey's plan to prosper the downtrodden Black folk. Now the conference was opposed to their efforts while they were not lifting a finger to help. "It just wasn't fair," they reasoned. No longer would they be oppressed. The hurt and outraged church members vocalized their grievances, but it seemed there was no resolution possible. No one seemed to be able to head off the impending storm. Pandemonium ensued. Either Humphrey would intervene and quiet things, or division was inevitable.

One thing was crystal clear: the Harlem congregation was solidly behind their pastor, Elder Humphrey. The conference officials felt they had to take action. They concluded that Humphrey and his church could not remain a part of the conference or the church and continue their plan. After hours of dialogue and

HUMPHREY SPEAKS

"In 1905 a brother came to my house and urged me to cut loose from this [Seventh-day Adventist] denomination. That man was about 20 years my senior. I flatly refused to do it. I had been only three years in the truth. I refused then to do it, and I refuse now to do it. . . . I told him that I had never seen in the Word of God a precedent for any man, under any circumstances whatever—of hardships and trials and troubles, of wrong treatment by his brethren—never a precedent for any man to turn aside from God's organized plan of work, and succeed. I therefore said, 'I cannot go with you'" (Elder James Humphrey, 1922 General Conference session).

debate, a resolution was made. The Greater New York Conference decreed that they drop the First Harlem church from its sisterhood of churches and that the former First Harlem church no longer be recognized as a Seventh-day Adventist church. Humphrey and his church were effectively disfellowshipped on January 14, 1930. The decision sent shock waves throughout the denomination. Never had the church seen anything like this case.

In retrospect, no one won or benefited from the split. The Seventh-day Adventist Church lost a sixth of its African-American members and one of its most charismatic, able Black leaders. Further, they lost the respect of many a careful observer who saw the church as highhanded and racist. Many Black Adventists were disillusioned by the events, and loyalties waned.

After the split, events didn't fare well for Humphrey, either. Soon his plan lost focus, languished, and fizzled. Finances were never adequate, and the enterprise met with opposition and legal difficulties. Rumors of money laundering and graft began to circulate, and an official investigation was carried out. The investigation, however, was concluded with: "no complaints of alleged wrongdoings had been brought to him [Humphrey]" and "no charges were pending against the promoters or anyone else connected with the association." But the bad press hung like a cloud over the project. Eventually all the money was returned to the investors. The plan was abandoned.

Since that time Humphrey's name has gone down in Adventist infamy. The congregation never returned to the Seventh-day Adventist Church. Neither did Humphrey. He is often viewed as self-serving, proud, and divisive. Many see the Utopia Park plan as Humphrey's attempt to garner personal power, personal gain, and personal prominence.

Yet these criticisms are questionable. Although God alone can judge the human heart, the cultural realities of the day suggest that there was more to the story. They suggest that the situation was complex and warrants closer examination.

First, Humphrey almost solely raised up the Harlem church, converting the approximately 600 individuals to the Seventh-day Adventist denomination. Only after the denomination disfellowshipped them were they under Humphrey's exclusive care. Second, Humphrey historically defended the Adventist Church and urged Blacks to never defect. He was expelled; he did not leave of his own behest. Next, Humphrey was never divisive toward the church. His Utopia Park scheme was in line with Adventism's standards and doctrines. Also, it was reported and affirmed by conference officials and members alike that Humphrey never spoke evil against the conference or conference workers. Finally, Humphrey was not dishonest with Utopia Park funds. He didn't earn a cent off of the endeavor. Most important is the fact that Humphrey, in his Utopia Park plan, was passionately committed to the development and upbuilding of Black people in the context of Adventism. Sensitivity to culture and conditions required a more understanding view of Humphrey and Utopia Park. Could it have been a good plan that each side went about addressing the wrong way?

James Humphrey can best be viewed in the context of his times. Facing tremendous pressure from all sides, he served as a mediator between the Black world and the world of Adventism. He tried to accommodate both sides until he felt he could no longer do so without doing damage to the hopes and aspirations of Black people. Most important is the realization that he never sought expulsion from God's church—he had converted hundreds of people to it. He left when he was put out, when he was required to do so. Humphrey was a leader, an advocate, a visionary. He was human with failings, yes, but committed to the gospel and the uplifting of humanity and the Black race.

Several blessings came from the Utopia mishap. The Seventh-day Adventist Church finally began to take a more serious view of the plight of Black Seventh-day Adventists. They began to note the overt discrimination in the church and to accept the reality that little was being done about it. Further, the issues highlighted in the Utopia incident enlightened the church as to the demographical need for the Black work to be widely carried out in the whole nation and the world, not only in the South. Also important, Utopia Park focused attention on the relevancy of the health message and Adventist doctrine as an effective package to uniquely uplift Black people, oppressed people, and all people in need. Finally, the events in Harlem paved the way for the regional conference system, which has been an effective tool in the hands of God for the building of the Black work in the Adventist Church.

God can take an unfortunate event and use it for the development of His work.

SUMMARY
- James Humphrey raises up two Seventh-day Adventist churches and is a key worker in the denomination.
- Humphrey speaks out plainly about the denomination's injustice toward Black people.
- Humphrey tries to help Blacks when the denomination does not move fast enough, making plans to start the Utopia Benevolent Association.

- The General Conference disfellowships Humphrey and his church because of a lack of collaboration with leaders.
- The Utopia plan fails, and the Seventh-day Adventist Church loses a sixth of its Black membership.

FOR FURTHER READING

Baker, Delbert. *Telling the Story*. Loma Linda, Calif.: Loma Linda University Press, 1996.

Reynolds, Louis. *We Have Tomorrow*. Hagerstown, Md.: Review and Herald Pub. Assn., 1984.

Seventh-day Adventist Encyclopedia. Washington, D.C.: Review and Herald Pub. Assn., 1976.

---

[1] L. K. Dickson to J. K. Humphrey, Aug. 13, 1929.

[2] J. K. Humphrey to L. K. Dickson, Aug. 20, 1929.

CHAPTER 11

Death in D.C.

1943: WASHINGTON, D.C

LUCY BYARD, A BLACK WOMAN ON THE BRINK OF DEATH,
WAS REFUSED TREATMENT AT AN ADVENTIST HOSPITAL
BECAUSE OF HER COLOR.

~

*"Inasmuch as ye have done it unto one of the least of these
my brethren, ye have done it unto me" (Matt. 25:40).*

"BYARD, LUCY."

The attendant read the name, then glanced up at the fair-skinned woman in front of him. She was an older woman with large glasses, a dark overcoat and hat, and a kind, grand-motherly look on her face. Despite suffering from an acute case of pneumonia, the woman had a pleasant look about her. The man standing next to her—most likely, her husband—was very light-skinned too. He also wore a hat and overcoat, and had an urgent look in his gray eyes that said his wife needed help immediately.

"Take her to the emergency room pronto," the attendant commanded the assistants under his jurisdiction who stood staring at the woman idly.

Lucy Byard was placed in a wheelchair and wheeled to

the emergency room. She sped past room after room of the hospital, her husband trying to keep up. The halls were the usual bland tan color, and the atmosphere was unusually calm for a hospital in the evening. This appeared to be their only emergency case at the time.

Byard and the assistants arrived at the emergency room, and she was wheeled to the bed and placed gently in it. Her husband stood by her side, grasping her hand and whispering to her that God would bring her through it. Nurses and assistants started to file in, rushing around grabbing things and asking Byard questions intermittently. Then the doctor walked in wearing the usual blue smock, an intelligent-looking man in his 40s.

NEITHER BLACK NOR WHITE

Lucille Byard and her husband, John Byard, were neither Black nor White. Back then they were referred to as Mulattoes—of mixed Black-and-White parentage.

While the doctor began to examine her, the front desk attendant looked over the admittance forms that gave Byard's vital statistics. He hadn't had time to study them thoroughly because of Byard's pressing condition; now he stood in the room in a corner scanning them for more information about her.

He'd done this a million times. He flew past the name, address, birth date, height, and weight. What the man saw next caused him to stop and his jaw to drop open. Under race in fine black ink was the word "Negro!"

The man called another attendant to take a look. He tried not to make too much of a commotion. The young woman he called hurried over, a curious expression on her face, wondering why he would stop her from working to come look at a form. When he pointed to the N word, her mouth also fell open. "Oh, no, we have to do something. This hospital cannot treat her," she said with instant finality.

The two attendants looked at each other for a moment. They couldn't believe this was happening. The man who made the discovery nervously called the doctor (who was busy with Byard), first in a weak voice, then a little louder.

The doctor shot an exasperated look toward the source of the noise and waved them off. He started to work on Byard again as if he hadn't heard anything.

But the attendant called him again. "It's urgent, Doc," the man explained plaintively.

The doctor rushed over, perturbed that he had been interrupted from working on a very sick woman. "What is it?" he demanded.

"Uh, doctor, there has been a mistake—"

"What kind of mistake?" the doctor interrupted. This had better be worth his time or these two would be in deep trouble.

"With Lucy Byard." The attendant pointed over to the ill woman. Nurses still swarmed all around her, and her husband stood a little away from the bustle with a prayerful look on his face.

"I don't understand; what problem is there with her?" The doctor was about to wheel around and begin his work again when the female attendant spoke up.

"She is a Negro!"

The doctor stopped short, perplexed. "She can't be. She looks White to me," he reasoned. He knew what White people looked like, and he knew what Black people looked like, and the woman on the bed looked White.

"Sir, it says so on the form she filled out." The woman pointed at the line for race.

The doctor's jaw tightened. He had begun to sweat profusely. He cast a look at the form on the bed now, not believing what was happening. He weighed his dilemma.

Should he follow the social mores of the day and refuse to treat a Black woman in a hospital for Whites, or should he follow the Hippocratic oath, which is often summaried as "First do no harm"?

He chose the former. "Then she must go! We don't treat Negroes here. Take her to Freedman's Hospital, across town." With that the doctor hurried out of the room, an inner conflict raging in his head.

The two attendants glanced at each other. Who would be the one to do the dirty work? The male attendant knew that he had to do it. This would be the hardest thing he'd ever done in his life.

He walked the length of the short room, thinking about what he would say the whole time. The nurses had mysteriously been alerted of the situation, and all but two had slipped out of the room. The attendant stepped next to Byard's bed. She was coughing and wheezing. He could see that she was near death. To discharge her would literally be to sign her death warrant. Her husband clutched his hat in his hands, fearing for his wife of many years. Pity filled the attendant's heart. He thought of his grandmother and how much he loved her. Then he remembered that Lucy Byard was Black.

DADDY AND NANA

Lucy and John Byard were loved by everyone who knew them and were referred to affectionately as Daddy and Nana. Both played instruments extremely well and were superb chefs.

"Mrs. Byard," he called in the same whisper he had used with the doctor.

No response. The sick woman lay on the bed apparently unconscious.

"Mrs. Byard," he said louder, summoning his strength.

He saw her lips move and heard a faint "Yes."

The female attendant had by now escorted Byard's husband from the room and informed him of the situation in the hall.

"Mrs. Byard, you have to be taken to another hospital."

"Why?" Lucy Byard asked desperately.

"Well, because you're . . . you're Black," the attendant managed.

"Son, I can't go like this! Please, we are all God's children. Please help me—I am near death." Byard was now looking in the eyes of the attendant, trying to appeal to his Christianity and humanity. Her eyes, large and beseeching, sought some sign of compassion in the man's face.

"Sorry, ma'am." He spoke with his head down; he could no longer look her in the face.

Mrs. Byard submitted meekly as the attendant helped her into a wheelchair. She didn't have the strength to protest. The attendant rolled her out into the hall, where her husband stood talking to the female attendant. He also looked resigned, as though he just had to accept his fate. It was a pitiful sight as the four trudged down the halls and corridors of the Washington Adventist Hospital. Although Lucy Byard was a longtime Adventist from Brooklyn, New York, she was the wrong skin color.

ADVENTISTS EVERYWHERE

The Byards were welcomed to Freedman's Hospital at Howard University by J. Mark Cox, a young doctor who had graduated from Loma Linda.

Lucy Byard and her husband took a taxi to the Freedman's Hospital at Howard University. The doctors at Freedman's were aghast to see her arrive in such a weak condition—from a sister medical facility. The medical personnel tried valiantly to save her, but to no avail. They threw their hands up in despair as she breathed her last. If only they'd had more time. The taxi ride, exposure, and the ensuing wait had been too much.

Lucy Byard was dead from pneumonia.

Black Adventists all over the country were stunned. This travesty took place in an Adventist hospital? One of their very own? It just couldn't be! What of the love and compassion believers are to have for humanity, especially one of the same faith? What of equality in Christ? What of the healing ministry of the Adventist Church? What of human dignity? It was all too much. Something had to be done. This was an overt act of racism perpetrated in one of Adventism's flagship medical institutions. Because Adventists followed prevailing racial discriminatory practices, a wonderful, loving Adventist believer was dead.

TITHES INTO THE STOREHOUSE

Blacks contributed hundreds of thousands of dollars yearly to the Adventist institutions that they were denied access to.

The Adventist Church was guilty of the whole gamut of racial inequities, from segregation in Adventist schools and churches, to Blacks being shut out of churches and deprived of fellowship, to positions in church employment held back from Blacks, to racial quotas in Adventist institutions—even the way money was allotted. The situation in Washington wasn't new; it was just the most blatant and conspicuous act of a longstanding policy of racism. The situation had grown from bad to worse—and now this. A cry rose up from Black ministers and laypersons alike. Action needed to be taken, and it needed to be taken immediately.

The Lucy Byard incident turned out to be the last tragedy that would occur before the church took decisive action and aggressively sought to address racial inequities. Shortly after this incident Black-administered conferences were instituted. Immediately things were done to set the regional conference system in motion. Although the Lucy Byard event was atrocious, God used it to serve His divine purpose.

SUMMARY
- Lucy Byard goes to a prominent Seventh-day Adventist sanitarium in Washington, D.C., and is refused treatment because she is Black.
- She dies because she is not treated promptly.
- There is an uproar of protest among Black Seventh-day Adventists because of an accrual of racial grievances.
- This incident results in the church's aggressively addressing racial inequities.
- This event spurs the decision to vote Black Seventh-day Adventist conferences into existence.

LIFE LESSONS
- Many times the worst injustices can occur among God's people.
- A church can come far in certain areas and yet lag behind in others.
- God can use these tragedies to wake people up to think of ways to remedy problems.
- Prejudice should be eradicated by the principles of God's Word and human decency.
- One person's courageous stand can make the difference between life and death.

FURTHER READING
Baker, Delbert. *Telling the Story*. Loma Linda, Calif: Loma Linda University Press, 1996.

Bull, Malcolm, and Keith Lockhart. *Seeking a Sanctuary: Seventh-day Adventists and the American Dream.* New York: Harper and Row Publishers, 1989.

Justiss, Jacob. *Angels in Ebony.* Toledo, Ohio: Jet Printing Services, 1975.

Reynolds, Louis. *We Have Tomorrow.* Hagerstown, Md.: Review and Herald Pub. Assn., 1984.

CHAPTER 12:

Trial to Triumph

1944: CHICAGO, ILLINOIS

ETHNIC INCIDENTS, DEMOGRAPHIC CONDITIONS,
AND ORGANIZATIONAL REALITIES CAUSED THE ADVENTIST
LEADERSHIP TO VOTE THE CREATION OF
BLACK-ADMINISTERED CONFERENCES.

~

*"God having provided some better thing for us, that they
without us should not be made perfect" (Heb. 11:40).*

THE MEETING ROOM of the Chicago Stevens Hotel
had standing room only. It was late in the day. The delegates had
engaged in hours of rigorous discussion and passionate speeches.
Still, obstacles and difficulties faced the attendees at every turn.

Now the room was still. Every eye focused on the
speaker standing at the microphone. This was the moment
that everyone had been waiting for.

"Mr. Chairman, I move that we accept the president's
recommendation for the creation of Black conferences in the
Seventh-day Adventist Church as previously outlined," the
speaker announced in a clarion pitch.

"Is there a second?" the chairman responded.

Several throughout the room intoned their seconds to
the motion.

The chairman went on. "Discussion?"

"All those in favor say aye."

Scores of ayes could be heard around the room.

"Any opposed, the same sign."

"The ayes have it!" It was unanimous.

For a millisecond all was quiet. Then a nervous applause broke out. A new era had dawned in the Seventh-day Adventist Church.

~ ~ ~

The decade of the 1940s was a turbulent one in America and in the Adventist Church. The United States was still recovering from the crippling Great Depression of the 1920s and the 1930s. At the same time, dramatic racial changes were taking place in the Adventist Church that would influence its demographic and organizational structure for decades to come.

America was engaged in a world war that seemed to have no end in sight. The first enemy attack on American soil occurred in 1941 when the Japanese attacked Pearl Harbor, Hawaii. This event plunged the nation into an atmosphere of anger and despair. By 1944 the Allied Powers had gained the ascendancy in the war. Hitler's Germany was soon to be overcome, and it was clear that there would be a new order of things.

Equally important for domestic race relations, thousands of battle-weary soldiers of all races were returning home in search of jobs, opportunities, and a new life. The Seventh-day Adventist Church, like the nation in general, had come to recognize the dilemma of race relations as a major issue needing attention; nevertheless, no significant breakthroughs had been realized. In many ways the church lagged behind the nation in the move toward racial equality.

A struggle continued within the Adventist Church as to how to deal with the race issue. In spite of Christ's appeal for unity in John 17, in spite of the hundreds of Bible references mandating love for one another, in spite of the hundreds of pages of inspired counsel on how to advance the work among Blacks, the Adventist Church continued to labor with the race question.

As the nation seemed ready to face its problems, the Adventist Church seemed determined to maintain the status quo. Denominational leadership positions remained virtually inaccessible to Black people. People of African descent were still discouraged from worshipping in most White congregations. Church institutions and facilities remained essentially segregated. Enrollment in White Adventist schools was still virtually unheard-of for Black children and youth.

In the years following Edson White's ministry, missionary outreach toward Blacks in the South had slowed to a crawl. Other denominations, such as the Catholics, Baptists, and Methodists, were far more active in their outreach efforts and humanitarian and educational work for Blacks in the South. In fact, in certain areas of the church there were whispers of the influence of White extremist groups.

Voices urging change in the Adventist Church—appeals for increased racial equality and inclusiveness—had been heard and ignored for decades. But the cruel and unnecessary death of Lucy Byard could not be ignored. This incident was the catalyst that brought the race relations conflict in the Adventist Church to a head. (See the previous chapter.) No person with a modicum of dignity could sit idly by and let events continue to unfold as they were.

Dedicated Black Adventists formed groups to study how to effect positive change, to better realize Christ's commission to take the gospel to all the world. These prayer and study groups were comprised mainly of laypersons, but pastors, Bible workers, and church employees were also present at these meetings. When they met, there was dialogue, debate, strategy, and prayer. Foremost on the agenda was the challenge of finding ways for the church to relate positively to the oppressed and disenfranchised while maintaining its God-given mission to the world.

With the injustices Blacks had suffered, the groups could have deteriorated into mere gripe sessions. They could have been contentious, focusing more on the problem than on solutions. But amazingly, they were not. In fact, a deliberate effort was made to avoid talk of abandoning the denomination or spreading discord. Instead, discussion focused on how to create positive change within the denomination. Participants loved the Adventist Church and wanted to see it reach its potential in Christ. Often they stayed up late at night.

Ellen White's statements, speeches, and actions on race issues were analyzed and found to be invaluable. Further, the work of Edson White was often referred to as "exhibit A" in group discussions. Edson had done everything humanly possible to evangelize the recently freed slaves in the South, and at great risk to himself and his family. His work and spirit served as a notable role model.

Other colorful personalities contributed to the race relations dialogue during this period. Charles Kinney, the tireless Black preacher often referred to as "the father of the Black work," was one of the first voices speaking up for Black conferences. William H. Green, the first secretary of the Negro Department, was an indefatigable advocate for the need of equity and rights for Blacks. Though he died suddenly in 1928, his efforts on behalf of his fellow Black believers gave direction to the movement. Scores of Black leaders during this period urged change and improvement.

The concept of Black-administered conferences began to gain real momentum. It was increasingly seen as a way for the Black Adventist work to progress, to allow for shared governance, and to provide opportunities for leadership growth and development.

So following the Byard tragedy, Black-administered conferences became more appealing, more viable. Black laypersons and leaders petitioned General Conference president James L. McElhany to take action and form conferences that would be led by Blacks in order to progress the work for Blacks more aggressively.

McElhany came to believe that finding a way to assist Black Adventists was a moral issue. Clearly he had to do something to remedy the situation. McElhany was sensitive and sympathetic to the plight of Black Adventists. He had posited earlier that Black conferences appeared to be one of the major ways Blacks could receive fair treatment to prosper the work among their people.

In 1944, in an unprecedented move, President McElhany agreed to address the issue of race relations in the church and the organization of Black conferences at the upcoming General Conference Spring Council. The meeting was to be held in Chicago, Illinois. The plan was that his address would deal with the pros and cons of Black-administered conferences and the merits of a plan to make them a reality. In preparation for the Spring Council, the General Conference Committee voted to invite leading Black leaders to the meeting. As the date approached, the church waited in anticipation.

~ ~ ~

April 8, 1944, the date for the beginning of Spring
Council, finally arrived. Meetings were held at the Stevens
Hotel in Chicago. From the outset of the council the atmosphere was tense. Outside, the blustery Chicago winds blew
furiously under the steel-gray sky.

For hours Black and White denominational leaders discussed the topic of Black-administered conferences and debated
the general concept. Attendants from all across the country discussed at length the emotionally
charged subject. Everyone knew
that something had to be done, but
what? And how and when? Was this
the right time? The attendees were
caught up in a supercharged organizational dilemma.

All day the leaders of the denomination discussed, debated, and
deliberated. The decision about
Black conferences was to be made
the next day when the president addressed the assembly. A
vote would be taken.

PAY YOUR WAY

*Several Black leaders who
attended the 1944 Spring
Council paid their
transportation cost to
Chicago. The hat was passed
to collect money to pay for
phone calls, ink for the
typewriter, and printing costs.*

The next morning, when it was time for General
Conference president McElhany to preside over the session,
he was not present. Consternation and confusion permeated
the session. What had happened? Where was the president?
Why was he absent? Would he come? The atmosphere grew
tense, marked by low whispers and perplexed looks. It
seemed that no one knew just what to do. All day the leaders of the denomination debated back and forth as to what
should be done. McElhany was nowhere in sight. He had

been stricken with sickness and lay in bed in his hotel room. He was so ill that he couldn't even get up, let alone preside over the proceedings.

Those in the meeting room were restless. Where was the president? Was he in an accident? Was he sick? Did he not think this gathering important? The atmosphere grew tense, marked by low whispers and perplexed looks. Action was demanded.

One of Black Adventism's premier leaders, George Peters, took the initiative to find out what was keeping the president. He arose from his seat and asked the men present to continue the meeting while he went to find out what the problem was. The men agreed, and Peters hurried to the president's hotel room. Through the halls, up the elevator, Peters was thinking and praying. Praying for the future of God's work and for the salvation of Black people.

A TRUE PIONEER SPEAKS

"I am not a radical. I am not an agitator. Nothing is accomplished without God. Pardon my personal reference, but I have, through the help of God, brought in about 3,000 souls. In one meeting I baptized 145 without stopping. . . . Who am I to say that we should have Colored conferences? Whatever it takes to bring classes of Negroes into this message, that is the thing that I am after. We must have greater evangelism" (G. E. Peters, 1944).

Peters gently knocked on the polished wooden door of the president's hotel suite and waited a couple of moments. He was escorted in by a nurse, who was tending to the president. The room was dark as the shades were drawn so the president could sleep. Peters was led to the president's bedside.

"Elder Peters, how are you?" the sick president asked in a tired voice, proffering his right hand. He was under several blankets, and only his head could be seen. He did look ill, his face drawn and his eyes weak.

"Good, Elder McElhany," replied Peters, warmly grasping the hand of the president. He looked sympathetically at the bedridden man.

"How are you feeling?" Peters asked.

"I felt really bad earlier, but I have been improving." The president seemed to gain strength as they talked.

Peters waited as long as was courteous and cordial before he got to the real point of his visit. He sat in a chair next to the president's bed, a prayer for wisdom still in his heart.

G. E. *Peters*

"Elder McElhany, the meeting has started. We need you out there. I know that you are sick, but I believe God will give you strength to make the session and present your address," Peters urged gently.

"Yes, I want to attend, and I planned to attend. But I fear that I might faint or worse out there," the president responded pensively. "I don't want that to happen." He knew that things in the denomination could not continue as they were. Something had to be done to alleviate the racial problems in the church, and he might be the one God would use to do it. Yet here he was sick in bed on the day of the meeting.

Peters continued: "Mr. President, the time is crucial. As you know, if a statement is to be made, now is the time to make it, to take a stand, to make it clear what you believe is the right thing to do. Elder, we are counting on you. If this moment passes, I fear the situation may deteriorate. If you don't address the group, I don't see how you could ever face the Black constituency again. You made a promise, and we are counting on you." Peters had to be forceful. The situation was that critical.

With resolve, the president marshaled his strength and sat up in bed. *Elder Peters is right,* McElhany thought. He had made a promise, and he must keep it. He had a duty to God, his church, and his colleagues.

The president breathed a prayer and put a leg on the floor. Then another. He stood in front of Peters and grasped the Black leader's hand once again. The two instantly knew that a prayer for wisdom and strength was in order, so both of them fell to their knees right then and there in the hotel room. After both had petitioned God, McElhany got up, dressed, and made his way to the meeting hall with Peters.

NO MORE RACISM

"The thing for us to do is to get this work finished just as soon as we can and go to our eternal home, where these racial conditions do not exist. It will be a glorious thing when we can go to our eternal home. We will forget all the things that have troubled us in this world" (J. L. McElhany, 1944).

Once in the hall, President McElhany carefully walked to the podium. He valiantly shook off illness and fatigue as he spoke his convictions bravely and powerfully. He treated both the evolution and needs of the Black work. He thoroughly covered both the concept of and the plan for the creation of Black conferences. Freely talking about his deep love and concern for the Black work, he also expressed his confidence in Black leadership. Finally, he let everyone present know in no uncertain terms that it was time to initiate Black conferences. Elder McElhany's address to the session was pointed and powerful. Its impact and outcome caused it to be viewed as one of the more effective speeches in Adventist history.

After McElhany's address, other prominent leaders stood

up to speak in favor of the creation of Black conferences. These leaders included such Adventist legends as W. A. Spicer, J. J. Nethery, F. L. Peterson, and W. W. Fordham.

The council attendees continued to dialogue about the rationale for Black conferences and the best way to bring about their creation. They articulated the following reasons:

Unique Needs: Black conferences were necessary because of the unique needs of Black Seventh-day Adventists. These needs entailed everything from evangelistic methods to access to medical and educational institutions, which were not being met adequately under the present conference system.

Neutralize Racism: Racism existed in the Adventist Church. The effect on all within its influence was negative. The Black conferences were seen as a way around that racism.

Facilitate Integration: Black conferences would encourage and nurture something that did not exist in the church—real integration. Regional conferences would allow for parity and equity. That is, Black conferences would be seen as equal to the White conferences in governance and priority. Further, under their auspices, Black leaders could be developed for leadership in the world church. Without Black conferences, Blacks would be hard pressed to obtain equal status.

Governance Voice: Black conferences would provide the Black membership with a natural and legitimate voice in denominational governance. The views and beliefs of the Black constituency could be sounded in a respectful and dignified forum without having to create an artificial avenue.

Effective Evangelism: African-Americans needed to be evangelized systematically and consistently in order to fulfill the gospel commission and the three angels' messages. This was not being done and could not be done effectively in the White conferences.

THE VOTE FOR REGIONAL CONFERENCES

After the speeches an attendee approached the microphone and stated simply, "I move that the president's recommendation for Black conferences be accepted." The idea was God-inspired, and met with widespread acceptance. Shortly after the motion the council unanimously voted that Black conferences be established with this pronouncement:

"Whereas, the present development of the work among the Colored people in North America has resulted, under the signal blessing of God, in the establishment of some 233 churches with some 17,000 members; and, whereas it appears that a different plan of organization for our Colored membership would bring further great advance in soul-winning endeavors; therefore we recommend, that in unions where the Colored constituency is considered by the union conference committee to be sufficiently large, and where the financial income and territory warrant, Colored conferences be organized."

WHY NOT BLACK CONFERENCES?

"In Europe we have German conferences, French conferences, Swedish and Polish conferences; why not Black conferences?" (former General Conference president William Spicer, 1944).

The Blacks present were not permitted to vote, so it was especially amazing that the idea was put into existence the way it was. Blacks everywhere breathed a sigh of relief once the news was out. Finally they were on the stretch of the road to equality in the body of Christ. Finally they were allowed the medium to develop the Black constituency and the Black work within the structure of the Seventh-day Adventist Church. Praise God!

CREATION OF REGIONAL CONFERENCES

Over a three-year period (1945-1947), seven presidents

and seven regional conferences began the organizational framework that later developed into the nine Black-administered conferences that exist today. The Black conferences were termed regional because they consisted of a mostly Black constituency and covered regional areas of the country in the territory of an already-existing union conference.

The rest is history. With the start of each new conference, able, innovative leaders were chosen to lead and pioneer the new entity.

The Lake Region Conference was established in 1945. Its first president was J. G. Dasent. Its territory was comprised of Wisconsin and parts of Minnesota, Illinois, Indiana, and Michigan.

The Northeastern Conference was established in 1945. Its first president was L. H. Bland. Its territory was comprised of Rhode Island, Ver-

First Black Presidents

mont, Massachusetts, New Hampshire, Maine, New York, and Connecticut.

The Allegheny Conference was established in 1945. Its first president was J. H. Wagner. Its territory included New Jersey, Ohio, Delaware, Washington, D.C., and parts of Pennsylvania, Maryland, and West Virginia.

The South Central Conference was established in 1946. Its first president was H. R. Murphy. Its territory included Mississippi, Alabama, Tennessee, Kentucky, and part of Florida.

The South Atlantic Conference was established in 1946. Its first president was H. D. Singleton. Its territory included South Carolina, North Carolina, Georgia, and most of Florida.

The Southwest Region Conference was established in 1947. Its first president was W. W. Fordham, Its territory included Texas, Oklahoma, New Mexico, Louisiana, and Arkansas.

The Central States Conference was established in 1947 (because its membership was below the standard for a conference, it was first designated a "mission"). Its first president was T. M. Rowe. Its territory included North Dakota, South Dakota, Nebraska, Missouri, Wyoming, Kansas, Iowa, Colorado, and a portion of New Mexico and Minnesota.

Membership of all of the Black conferences grew steadily. Because these were area conferences covering multiple states instead of comprising a single state, as did the White conferences, this growth made further organizational changes inevitable. In 1967 the Allegheny Conference was divided into the Allegheny East Conference and the Allegheny West Conference. The first president of the Allegheny East Conference was W. A Thompson. Its territory was comprised of New Jersey, Delaware, Washington, D.C., and parts of Pennsylvania, Maryland, and Virginia. The first president of the Allegheny West Conference was W. M. Starks. Its territory included Ohio, West Virginia, and parts of Maryland, Pennsylvania, and Virginia.

The South Atlantic Conference was divided in 1981, forming the South Atlantic Conference and the Southeastern Conference. The first president of the Southeastern Conference was James Edgecombe. Its territory included southern Georgia and Florida. At the time of the division the officers of the South Atlantic Conference were retained. Its territory then included South Carolina, North Carolina, and part of Georgia.

TRIAL TO TRIUMPH

In the years that followed the historic beginnings of the regional conferences, God provided able, talented African-American leaders to the Seventh-day Adventist Church through the regional conferences. These persons are spread throughout the leadership structure of the national and world church.

Regional conferences have met and are still meeting the outlined needs and purposes for their existence, as outlined in 1944. Among their most notable contributions to the church are the great advance in membership through successful soul winning and the erection of churches, schools, and other resources.

The membership of Black Seventh-day Adventists was around 17,000 in 1944 when the regional conferences were first established. Since then, under the auspices of regional conference leaders, Black membership in the United States

CAN'T BEAT GOD GIVING

Currently tithe returns from regional conferences exceed the annual tithe returns of every world division except the North American Division.

has mushroomed to approximately 300,000, with a $150 million tithe base. With the exception of the North American Division, the annual tithe from regional conferences exceeds the total tithe of any other division in the world field.

Regional (Black) conferences were born in the midst of the trials of racial challenges, leadership needs, and evangelism necessities. As a result, God took this trial and turned it into a triumph not only for the progress of the Black Adventist work but also for the triumph of the worldwide work of the Adventist Church. To God be the glory!

SUMMARY

- Racial tensions, ethnic leadership needs, and critical mass conditions in the church force Adventist leaders to face the need for Black-administered conferences.

- Black and White laypersons and leaders create a catalyst to improve racial conditions in the church.
- General Conference president J. L. McElhany and other church leaders support the formation of regional conferences in 1944.
- Regional conferences are officially voted into existence in 1944, and seven of the current nine conferences are formed from 1945 to1947.
- Regional conferences are a success story, demonstrating that with God's providence, an apparent trial can be transformed into a triumph.

LIFE LESSONS

- Crisis can be the catalyst for creative change.
- Every entity has its own history and background that must be factored in to understand where it is and where it is going.

FURTHER READING

Baker, Delbert. *Telling the Story*. Loma Linda, Calif.: Loma Linda University Printing Service, 1996.

Brownstone, David, and Irene Franck. *Timelines of the 20th Century*. New York: Little Brown and Company, 1996.

Fordham, W. W. *Righteous Rebel*. Hagerstown, Md.: Review and Herald Pub. Assn., 1990.

Justiss, Jacob. *Angels in Ebony*. Toledo. Ohio: Jet Printing Service, 1990.

Rock, Calvin, ed. *Perspectives*. Hagerstown, Md.: Review and Herald Pub. Assn., 1996.

Seventh-day Adventist Encyclopedia. Washington, D.C.: Review and Herald Pub. Assn., 1976.

AFTERWORD

Of ancient Israel we read, "Now all these things happened unto them for ensamples: and they are written for our admonition, upon whom the ends of the world are come" (1 Cor. 10:11). This verse is representative of Paul's constant references to ancient Israel. He wished to impart real-life lessons to his churches, and he appealed to the experience of their ancestors. Peter did the same thing, as did John, Jude, Stephen, and our Lord and Savior Jesus Christ. These instruction-filled stories spoke poignantly to the fledgling Christian church and gave them encouragement, counsel, and warning.

The similarities between ancient Israel and African-Americans are provocative. Both were enslaved for 400 years and subjected to extreme humiliation and forced toil. Both were enslaved in lands foreign to them. Both groups endured the rigors of slavery through their faith in God. Inspiration reveals that God expressly and personally freed both groups.

After their emancipation, both groups had to struggle to live in a world that was free yet antagonistic toward them. God revealed His truth to the Israelites and to African-Americans, teaching them His commandments and grace. As a result, both groups were restored and became respected worldwide because of their adherence to these laws.

How quickly we read the Old Testament stories of Israel and draw lessons for our lives but yet totally ignore the experience of African-Americans! This is even more startling when we realize that we do not serve an evolutionary-type God who sets the earth in motion and lets it run without interposing, nor do we serve a God who worked in ancient times but ceased activities after Bible times. No, we serve a God who has been equally active at all points in history.

History is invaluable to us for several reasons. First, it makes us aware of the character and experiences of our ancestors: their strengths and weaknesses, triumphs and defeats. Second, it gives us insight as to the nature of the world and of humanity. Third, it provides focus and instruction for the future. Last but most important, it shows us that we serve a God who is intimately involved in the affairs of people. This is especially true of Seventh-day Adventist history. In these chapters we see a God who is active. In each narrative, divine Providence can be seen guiding and directing both events and people behind the scenes. We realize that Jehovah works through men and women like us, irrespective of their faults, idiosyncrasies, and broken promises. Ultimately, God's will must be done.

The reader is challenged by these stories because the end of the world has come upon us. Our mission is clearly outlined in God's Word: to go and preach the gospel to the world. The lessons are clear: if we give ourselves wholly to God's work, He will give us success in our endeavors, despite all obstacles and odds. Our mission is not impossible; with God it is very possible.

We've read about the others—now it is our turn.

LIST OF RESOURCES

Baker, Delbert. *Make Us One*. Boise, Idaho: Pacific Press Publishing Association, 1995.

————. *Telling the Story*. Loma Linda, Calif : Loma Linda University Printing Services, 1996.

————. *The Unknown Prophet*. Hagerstown, Md.: Review and Herald Pub. Assn., 1987.

Bennett, Lerone. *Before the Mayflower: A History of the Negro in America*. New York: Penguin Books, 1966.

Brownstone, David, and Irene Franck. *Timelines of the 20th Century*. New York: Little, Brown and Company, 1996.

Bull, Malcolm, and Keith Lockhart. *Seeking a Sanctuary: Seventh-day Adventists and the American Dream*. New York: Harper and Row Publishers, 1989.

Burner, David. *The American People*. St. James, N.Y.: Stoney Brook Press, 1980.

Chilson, Adrian. *They Had a World to Win*. Hagerstown, Md.: Review and Herald Pub. Assn., 2001.

Coon, Roger. *The Great Visions of Ellen G. White*. Hagerstown, Md.: Review and Herald Pub. Assn., 1992.

Dudley, Charles. *"Thou Who Hast Brought Us."* Brushton, N.Y.: Teach Services, Inc., 1997.

————. *Thou Who Hast Brought Us Thus Far on Our Way*. Mansfield, Ohio: Bookmasters, Inc, 2000.

Fordham, W. W. *Righteous Rebel*. Hagerstown, Md.: Review and Herald Pub. Assn., 1990.

Franklin, John Hope. *From Slavery to Freedom*. New York: Alfred A. Knopf Inc., 1980.

Graybill, Ronald. *E. G. White and Church Race Relations*. Washington, D.C.: Review and Herald Pub. Assn., 1970.

————. *Mission to Black America*. Washington, D.C.: Review and Herald Pub. Assn. 1971.

Heidler, David, ed. *Encyclopedia of the American Civil War: A Political, Social, and Military History*. New York: W. W. Norton and Company, 2002.

Horton, James. *Black Bostonians*. New York: Holmes and Meier, 1979.

Hummel, Jeffrey. *Emancipating Slaves, Enslaving Free Men: A History of the American Civil War*. New York: Open Court Publishing Company, 1996.

Justiss, Jacob. *Angels in Ebony*. Toledo, Ohio: Jet Printing Services, 1975.

Knight, Anna. *Mississippi Girl*. Nashville, Tenn.: Southern Pub. Assn., 1952.

Knight, George. *Walking With Ellen White*. Hagerstown, Md.: Review and Herald Pub. Assn., 1999.

Leckie, Robert. *The Wars of America*. New York: HarperCollins Publishers, Inc., 1992.

Loughborough, John. *The Great Second Advent Movement*. Washington, D.C.: Review and Herald Pub. Assn., 1905.

Marshall, Norwida and Steven Norman III, eds. *A Star Gives Light*. Decatur, Ga.: Southern Union Conference of Seventh-day Adventists, 1989.

Maxwell, Mervyn. *Tell It to the World*. Boise, Idaho: Pacific Press, 1977.

Oakwood College *Fact Book 2002-2003*. Huntsville, Ala.: Office of Institutional Effectiveness. Oakwood College.

Reynolds, Louis B. *We Have Tomorrow*. Hagerstown, Md.: Review and Herald Pub. Assn., 1984.

Rock, Calvin, ed. *Perspectives*. Hagerstown, Md.: Review and Herald Pub. Assn., 1996.

Schwarz, Richard. *Light Bearers*. Nampa, Idaho: Pacific Press, 2000.

Sepulveda, Ciro, ed. *Ellen White on the Color Line*. Huntsville, Ala.: Biblos Press, 1997.

―――. *The Ladies of Oakwood*. Huntsville, Ala.: Oakwood College Press, 2003.

Seventh-day Adventist Encyclopedia. Washington, D.C.: Review and Herald Pub. Assn., 1976.

Simpson, Fred. *The Sins of Madison County*. Huntsville, Ala.: Triangle Publishing Co., 2000.

Spalding, Arthur. *Origin and History of Seventh-day Adventists*. Washington D.C.: Review and Herald Pub. Assn., 1962. Vols. 1, 2.

"Story of Anna Knight." As told to A. W. Spalding in Atlanta, Ga., Nov. 19, 22, 1914, Ellen G. White Estate Document File 372-1, 1914.

Warren, Mervyn. *Oakwood! A Vision Splendid*. Collegedale Tenn.: College Press, 1996.

White, Arthur. *Ellen G. White: The Lonely Years*. Hagerstown, Md.: Review and Herald Pub. Assn., 1984. Vol. 3.

White, Ellen. *Testimonies for the Church*. Mountain View, Calif.: Pacific Press Pub. Assn., 1948. Vols. 1, 5, 7, 9.

―――. *The Southern Work*. Washington, D.C.: Review and Herald Pub. Assn., 1966.